How University Budgets Work

How University Budgets Work

Dean O. Smith

Johns Hopkins University Press • *Baltimore*

© 2019 Johns Hopkins University Press
All rights reserved. Published 2019
Printed in the United States of America on acid-free paper
9 8 7 6 5 4 3 2 1

Johns Hopkins University Press
2715 North Charles Street
Baltimore, Maryland 21218-4363
www.press.jhu.edu

Library of Congress Cataloging-in-Publication Data

Names: Smith, Dean O., 1944- author.
Title: How university budgets work / Dean O. Smith.
Description: Baltimore : Johns Hopkins University Press, [2019] |
    Series: Higher ed leadership essentials | Includes bibliographical
    references and index.
Identifiers: LCCN 2019001855 | ISBN 9781421432762 (pbk. : alk. paper) |
    ISBN 9781421432779 (electronic) | ISBN 1421432765 (pbk. : alk. paper) |
    ISBN 1421432773 (electronic)
Subjects: LCSH: Universities and colleges—United States—Finance. |
    Universities and colleges—United States—Accounting. | Education,
    Higher—United States—Administration. | Education, Higher—Management.
Classification: LCC LB2342 .S555 2019 | DDC 378.1/06—dc23
    LC record available at https://lccn.loc.gov/2019001855

A catalog record for this book is available from the British Library.

*Special discounts are available for bulk purchases of this book. For more information,
please contact Special Sales at 410-516-6936 or specialsales@press.jhu.edu.*

Johns Hopkins University Press uses environmentally friendly book materials,
including recycled text paper that is composed of at least 30 percent post-
consumer waste, whenever possible.

Contents

PREFACE   vii

1 The Language of Budgets   1

2 University Budgets   18

3 Budget Models   47

4 Strategic Plans   73

5 Operating Budget Preparation   89

6 Budget Implementation   110

7 End of the Fiscal Year   136

8 Power of the Budget   153

NOTES   171

INDEX   177

Preface

As planets revolve around the sun, universities revolve around the budget. Indeed, budgets form the core of the academic enterprise. Few things happen if they're not somehow included in the budget. Therefore, to understand how universities work, it is critical to understand how their budgets work.

To enable this understanding, *How University Budgets Work* provides a concise explanation of all major aspects of university budgets. Topics range from the principles of budgetary accounting to the procedures for implementing the budget at the department level. Pedagogically, the book is written with no presumption of familiarity with university accounting or finance. Throughout, it emphasizes practical matters: logical rationales, best practices, and useful advice. Technical jargon is translated into commonly used terms, and basic principles are interpreted in an academic context. Sample budgets illustrate key concepts, making it easy to follow the accounting arithmetic. Ultimately, the aim is to develop a working knowledge of university budgets: how they are produced and implemented.

This introductory book derives from its more rigorous predecessor, *University Finances: Accounting and Budgeting Principles for Higher Education* (Johns Hopkins University Press, 2019). Some portions of that book have been expanded in *How University Budgets Work*, but the approach in this book is less quantitative and less technical. In fact, the two books were written for different audiences.

How University Budgets Work is written primarily for the members of the extended academic community. As an introductory reference book, it is intended for an audience that includes students, faculty, staff, administrators, governing board members, and anyone else who deals directly or indirectly with universities. Most probably, it would particularly interest new administrators who want to expand their understanding of higher education budgeting. In that regard, this book is ideally suited for one-day workshops and retreats on university budgets.

For students of higher education, this book could serve as a textbook for introductory courses on higher education administration and management. These courses are generally required for graduate students studying higher education. Moreover, it could serve as a basic textbook for courses and seminar series on higher education finances.

In the first chapter, the accounting terms used when describing budgets are defined. The goal is to introduce the words and explain their meaning. The second chapter introduces university budgets. After defining the characteristics of a budget in a university context, the distinguishing features of three principal types of university budgets are presented: auxiliary, capital, and operating. In addition, the concept of position budgets is introduced. Chapter 3 describes the various budget models used to allocate revenue and discusses the pros and cons of each model.

The next four chapters present the procedures for preparing and implementing the operating budget. Chapter 4 presents the foundation for budget preparation, the strategic plan. Then, in chapter 5, the budget preparation process, including revenue and expenditure projections, is described in detail. With the budget in place, its implementation is presented in chapter 6, which introduces the concept of budget variances and answers questions about how universities accommodate budget over- and underspending. Chapter 7 explains the steps involved in closing the budget at the end of a fiscal year.

The final chapter, chapter 8, explores the power of the budget. It discusses the importance of money in the university context and the budget's role as an agent of change. The book concludes with an analysis of the legal and contractual nature of the budget.

I wish to acknowledge Greg Britton and the editorial staff at Johns Hopkins University Press. They provided the inspiration and technical help needed to produce this book.

In addition, I wish to thank all of my colleagues who have contributed helpful comments about various aspects of this project. In particular, I thank Ray Pinner (University of Alabama in Huntsville) and Curtis Smith (California State University, Sacramento), who reviewed the manuscript for relevance and accuracy. Foremost, I thank Karlene Hoo (Gonzaga University), who reviewed the manuscript and provided invaluable advice, encouragement, and support along the way. Finally, I acknowledge my beagle, Barney, who unknowingly provided soothing companionship while lying faithfully by my side as I worked on this book.

How University Budgets Work

Chapter 1

The Language of Budgets

As the newly appointed chair of the history department, Professor T assumed new responsibilities. Some of them involved familiar concepts: make teaching assignments, review the curriculum, appoint committee members, and coordinate faculty meetings. Others involved vaguely familiar concepts: conduct performance evaluations, respond to grievances, and prepare for accreditations. They could be understood with minimal effort.

One responsibility in particular involved foreign concepts: the budget. Initially, Professor T thought, "Can it be so difficult to understand how the budget works? Surely, the departmental fiscal officer can explain it to me." But as the first year wore on, the budget proved more difficult to master than Professor T had originally thought. In fact, just communicating with the fiscal officer about budget matters was difficult at times. The fiscal officer's vocabulary contained familiar words, but in the context of budgets they referred to elusive concepts, such as ledger posting, unfavorable variances, and liquidated encumbrances. In short, when it came to understanding how budgets work, Professor T encountered an unexpectedly steep learning curve.

As Professor T discovered, to understand university budgets, it helps to know the language of budgets. What words are used, and what do they mean in the budgetary context? Therefore, this first chapter answers these questions. Pedagogically, the goal is to impart a basic familiarity with the vocabulary of budgeting. Although this way of introducing budgets may seem pedantic at first, its aim is to deliver the tools needed to take a look under the hood.

Accounting Terminology

A handful of basic financial terms appear over and over again in accounting: revenue and expenditures, accounts, journals and ledgers, debits and credits. For some of these terms, the accounting meanings are about the same as in everyday parlance. For others, however, the meanings are less familiar because they are not used ordinarily. So, for clarity, the most commonly used accounting terms will be defined more specifically in the context of budgets.

Fiscal Year

Budgets and other financial account records are organized into specific time periods. The basic period, the accounting time period, is the *fiscal year*, often abbreviated as FY. This may be the calendar year or some other one-year period. For example, the federal government's fiscal year runs from October 1 through September 30. Many universities' fiscal year runs from July 1 through June 30. Significantly, fiscal years are denoted by their end date. So if the fiscal year is the calendar year, FY 2020 runs from January 1, 2020, through December 31, 2020. For the federal government, FY 2020 runs from October 1, 2019, through September 30, 2020. And for the examples in this book, FY 2020 runs from July 1, 2019, through June 30, 2020.

Assets and Liabilities

In its simplest sense, an *asset* refers to "what you own." In the more nuanced accounting lexicon, "an asset is an item of economic value that is expected to yield a benefit to the owning entity in future periods."[1] An asset can be either short term or long term. A short-term asset lasts less than one fiscal year. Tuition revenue is an example of a short-term asset. Typically, it is spent within a fiscal year. In contrast, a long-term asset lasts more than one accounting period. Office buildings and machinery are examples of long-term assets.

A *liability* refers to "what you owe." In the accounting lexicon, "a liability is a legally binding obligation payable to another entity."[2] Liabilities are incurred to pay for the ongoing activities of the university. Examples of liabilities are accounts payable, wages payable, and taxes. These obligations are eventually settled by a university through the transfer of cash or other assets to some other party, such as a vendor or an employee. Like assets, liabilities can be either short term or long term. Liabilities the university expects to settle within one fiscal year, such as a credit card accounts payable, are short term; they are called current liabilities. All other liabilities, such as bank loans, are usually paid off over multiple years and are classified as long-term liabilities.

The term *net assets* refers to the difference between assets and liabilities. In equation form,

Net Assets = Assets – Liabilities.

Positive net assets indicate that the university can pay its debts. In contrast, negative net assets indicate that the university cannot possibly pay its debts; it is bankrupt. By the way, rearrangement of this equation yields the *fundamental accounting equation* for nonprofit organizations, including universities:

Assets = Liabilities + Net Assets.

Assets, liabilities, and net assets are reported on a specific date, usually the last day of a fiscal year. The reported values thus represent a snapshot of the university's financial condition on that day.

Revenues and Expenditures

Simply speaking, *revenues* refer to money taken in. More formally, revenue is money or another resource of value earned from providing products or services, resulting in an increase in assets. Thus, tuition paid to the university represents revenue earned from providing instruction. The single major difference between revenue and assets is that revenue is recorded over the course of a time period, such as an entire fiscal year, whereas assets are measured at a point in time, usually the last day of a fiscal year. For example, the university took in $1 million in tuition *revenue* during fiscal year 2020, and it held $10 million in cash *assets* on June 30, 2020.

Conversely, *expenditures* refer to money going out. More formally, an expenditure represents an outflow of money for the purpose of making a payment. It is a disbursement of cash, such as an employee's paycheck; money changes hands. Incidentally, the related term "expenses" represents not only disbursements but also consumption, or using up, of an asset. For example, payments for routine items such as office supplies or travel reimbursement are expenditures. Acquisitions of buildings and major equipment items are not expenditures. The cost of those items is recognized as an expense through depreciation over multiple years. In that sense, expenditures are a logical subset of expenses.

Net revenue refers to the difference between revenue and expenditures. In equation form,

Net Revenue = Revenue − Expenditures.

Revenue and expenditures are generally reported in real time. The values represent activities up to the date of the report.

There are two ways of classifying expenditures: natural and functional. In the natural classification scheme, expenditures are sorted by type—that is, by the nature of the expense. In the words of the Financial Accounting Standards Board (FASB), natural classification sorts expenses "according to the kinds of economic benefits received in incurring those expenses. Examples of natural expense classifications include salaries and wages, employee benefits, supplies, rent, and utilities."[3] In the functional classification scheme, expenses are sorted by function. According to the FASB, functional classification is "a method of grouping expenses according to the purpose for which costs are incurred. The primary functional classifications are program services and supporting activities."[4] Succinctly, natural classifications tell what was purchased, and functional classifications tell why it was purchased.

Within these two classification schemes, the National Association of College and University Business Officers (NACUBO) recommends the natural and functional expense classifications listed in table 1.1.[5] Most university budgets list expenditures according to their natural classification.

TABLE 1.1. *NACUBO-recommended expenditure classifications*

Natural	Functional
Salaries and wages	Instruction
Employee benefits	Research
Scholarships and fellowships	Public service
Travel	Academic support
Supplies	Student services
Utilities	Institutional support
Other outside services	Operations and maintenance (O&M)
Depreciation	Auxiliary and self-supporting enterprises
Interest	Hospitals
Other	Independent operations

Note: NACUBO = National Association of College and University Business Officers.

Accounts

Accounts are the elementary unit of a financial system. According to the dictionary, an *account* is "a record or statement of financial expenditure and receipts relating to a particular period or purpose."[6] The key concept lies in the words "relating to a particular period or purpose." The period is a fiscal year. The purpose can be any specific aspect of the university's operations: tuition, faculty salaries, graduate student stipends, repairs and maintenance, and so on. For example, a faculty salary account is simply a record of all expenditures relating to faculty salaries; a tuition account is a record of all receipts (that is, revenue) relating to tuition. In everyday experience, an individual might have a checking account, which is a record of all cash deposits and expenditures that are accessible easily by deposit slip and check.

Because of their myriad activities, universities usually have many accounts. Each account is for a particular activity or purpose, ranging from the general (for example, tuition) to the specific (for example, undergraduate air travel to a field station in Panama). Furthermore, an account may have numerous subaccounts, depending on the information desired. For example, a university might break down an equipment account into more specific subaccounts, such as centrifuges, x-ray equipment, and microscopes, depending on the resolution needed. In addition, every grant or contract from an external sponsor is usually assigned a unique account number. From that perspective, it is easy to comprehend that universities may have a large number of accounts, often numbering in the thousands.

Most institutions group their accounts into five basic account types:

- asset
- liability
- net assets

- revenue
- expense

Within each type, there are many different accounts. For example, asset accounts include operating cash, payroll cash, petty cash, and other accounts representing things owned by the university that have monetary value. Liability accounts include accounts payable, bank loans, credit card accounts, and other accounts representing money owed by the university. And so forth for the other three types.

Events that cause a change in an account are called *transactions*. The changes usually involve money taken in or paid out of the account. To keep track of these transactions, they must be recorded somehow as entries into the financial records, the "books." That is the responsibility of accountants.

Debits and Credits

Debits and credits refer to entries recording changes in account values as a result of a transaction. The terms are used conjointly in standard financial accounting because every financial transaction affects at least two different accounts. This concept comes from the basic accounting equation. Two simple examples illustrate this point. On the one hand, when the university receives $1 million in tuition revenue, its cash assets increase by $1 million. Therefore, the transaction affects both the revenue and cash accounts. On the other hand, when the university pays $1 million in faculty salaries, its cash assets decrease by $1 million and faculty salary liabilities decrease by $1 million. The transaction affects both the cash and the salary expense accounts.

To record the two entries resulting from this transaction, standard accounting practices worldwide use what is known as *double-entry accounting*, where each transaction entails entries in at least two different accounts. Historically in double-entry accounting, the accounting profession has recorded a transaction in two columns. By convention, the left column is known as the *debit* side and the right column is known as the *credit* side. Thus, making an entry on the left and the right sides is called debiting and crediting the account, respectively. Notably, this recording format uses only positive numbers. The "plus and minus" aspect of any transaction is preserved in the two-column, debit-credit method. Debit entries increase asset or expense accounts and decrease liability, net assets, or revenue accounts. Credits do the opposite: decrease asset and expense accounts and increase liability, net assets, and revenue accounts. Indeed, debits and credits are mirror images of each other. Returning to the examples above, when the university receives $1 million in tuition revenue, the tuition revenue account is credited $1 million and the cash assets account is debited $1 million. Conversely, when the university pays $1 million in faculty salaries, the cash assets account is credited $1 million and the faculty salary liabilities account is debited $1 million.

In double-entry accounting, every debit that is recorded must be matched with a credit. Actually, more than two accounts can be used if the transaction is spread among them, just as long as the sum of debits for the transaction equals the sum of credits for it. In other words, total debits and credits must be equal in every accounting transaction. That is,

Transaction Debits = Transaction Credits.

Although debits must equal credits for every transaction, the sum of all debits need not be equal to the sum of all credits for every individual account. Because the debits or credits for a transaction may be spread among several accounts, some accounts may receive more debits (or credits) than others. For each account, the difference between the sum of the debits and the sum of the credits is called the *balance*. The balance is called a debit balance if the sum of the debits exceeds the sum of the credits, and vice versa. Each account generally has either a debit balance or a credit balance, depending on the account type. Importantly, however, when total debits and credits for *all* accounts in the books are added up, total debits must equal total credits. If they do not, there must be a mistake in the accounting.

Nowadays, modern accounting software programs sidestep the need to identify the debits and credits involved in double-entry accounting when recording transactions. That process usually occurs automatically. Pragmatically, then, detailed knowledge about double-entry accounting is not necessary to understand how budgets work. Still, familiarity with at least the basic terminology can be handy, because some software applications refer to the underlying debits and credits on the computer screen as they automatically record budget transactions.

Journals and Ledgers

Modern accounting software also sidesteps two other aspects of recording transactions: journal entries and ledger posting. Nonetheless, they will be summarized here because the terms are still used in some settings. In earlier times, transactions were recorded chronologically in two sequential steps. The first step was a simple list: transactions were recorded sequentially in a journal as *journal entries*. Money taken in or paid out was designated as either a debit or a credit, respectively, by being placed in the debit or the credit column. Thus, the journal contained a chronological record of every economic transaction involving an account. These entries were accompanied by supporting records noting the details of each transaction for record-keeping and auditing purposes. Only individuals certified by the chief financial officer (CFO), such as fiscal officers, had the authority to make these entries. Because a journal entry was the first record of an account transaction, the journal was the so-called *book of original entry*.

At the journal-entry stage, the transaction was not assigned to particular accounts. That assignment occurred when journal entries were transferred—*posted* in accounting terms—into a ledger, which organized the transactions into the appropriate accounts. The ledger was known appropriately as the *book of second entry.* The journal and the ledger can be visualized as two notebooks, with the transactions arranged in double-entry format according to either the time when they occurred (the journal) or the account to which they apply (the ledger).

As noted, most accounting software programs now post transactions to the ledger automatically. This development has made the entire concept of a journal obsolete, and the term is seldom used. The concept of the ledger, however, remains in common use in financial accounting.

The main ledger, known as the *general ledger,* is the official record of the university's financial transactions. Maintained by the CFO, it includes all revenue and expenditure transactions, as well as balance sheets, for every account. Accordingly, financial accounting reports are derived from information in the general ledger. Some institutions also maintain subsidiary ledgers for specific aspects of the university's operations, such as grants and contracts and auxiliary services (for example, athletics and dining halls). These subsidiary ledgers usually contain more detail than the general ledger but fewer transactions. Importantly, information in these subsidiary ledgers feeds into the general ledger.

Trial Balances

Modern accounting software has automated another accounting practice, the *trial balance.* Since debits equal credits for each transaction, the total of all debit entries in the ledger should equal the total of all credit entries in the ledger. Historically, accountants would check for this equality by preparing periodic trial balances. In a two-column format, they listed the debit and credit balances for every account, added up the debit and credit columns, and compared the totals. Nowadays, accounting software makes sure that all debits and credits are in balance in real time whenever a transaction is processed.

Whether a trial balance is calculated by hand or by computer, if the total debits and credits agree, the trial balance is in balance, consistent with accuracy of the records. If the totals do not agree, the trial balance is not in balance, indicating that an error has occurred and must be located. Errors arise from failure to make all entries for a transaction. Notably, however, the trial balance is not foolproof. For example, recording the same transaction twice or posting a debit or credit to the wrong account would produce a balanced—but incorrect—trial balance. Thus, while a balanced trial balance does not necessarily guarantee accuracy, an unbalanced trial balance definitely indicates an error.

Budgetary Accounting

The term *budgetary accounting* is defined as "a method of accounting in which the amounts that a company planned to spend and the amounts it really spent are included in the accounts, so that you can see how much of the budget is left."[7] The key word is "planned." It refers to the forward-looking aspect of a budget. In that sense, budgetary accounting differs from financial accounting, which looks backward at income and expenditures already received and incurred, respectively.

In contrast to financial accounting, there are no generally accepted accounting principles (GAAPs) for budgetary accounting. Some states have established principles for state agencies, including public universities. For the most part, however, budgetary accounting principles are determined primarily by the university to suit its particular planning needs. Despite the lack of formal guidelines, university budgets generally adhere to a fairly standard format that lists at a minimum the estimated revenues and planned expenditures.

Importantly, most universities use what is known in the accounting profession as a *cash basis* of accounting when constructing their budgets. Under the cash basis, the university records (*recognizes* in accounting parlance) revenues when cash is received and expenditures when bills are paid. Thus, cash accounting is based on the underlying cash inflows or outflows; revenues and expenditures are recognized only when cash is received or paid, irrespective of the timing of actual services, sales, or purchases. This is an easy approach to recording transactions and is widely used owing to its simplicity. The cash basis also has practical advantages. It ensures that cash is available to pay for any expenditure. This favors the maintenance of a balanced budget, which is mandatory for many public institutions. Conversely, the university is not required to have cash available to pay for an expenditure that is deferred, such as a payout for unused vacation when an employee resigns or retires. This frees up revenue for other current needs.

Fund Accounting

Universities follow the principles of *fund accounting*. The practice of fund accounting originates from the need to account for revenues received from many different sources—donors, government agencies, grants and contracts, and so forth. Each source may stipulate its own specific restrictions or limitations on the use of its money. Therefore, universities must somehow keep tabs on the management of revenue from these various sources. They must focus on accountability. Is the money being spent according to the stipulations of donors, foundations, or the federal and state governments?

To accomplish this accountability, universities assign their cash resources to *funds* according to the stipulations placed on their use by the resource providers. For example, a federal grant to study autism and a gift to support undergraduate study abroad will have very different spending guidelines. Therefore, they are placed in two separate funds. Within each fund, there are a series of accounts (assets, liabilities, net assets, revenue, and expense) specific to that fund. So each fund is a separate accounting entity with its own set of books to ensure compliance with the limitations and restrictions placed on the use of its resources.

Note that the word "fund" has two additional meanings. In everyday parlance, it refers to "A sum of money saved or made available for a particular purpose" and to "Provide with money for a particular purpose."[8] The intended meaning is generally easy to decipher in context. Potential ambiguities will be clarified.

Chart of Accounts

To keep track of the many funds and accounts, an identifying number is assigned to each transaction as it is entered into the financial system. Information about the transaction is encoded in this number. At a minimum, this number encodes basic fund and account information, such as

- fund group
- function code (instruction, research, public service, and so forth)
- funding source code
- department
- project indicator (for example, a federal grant identification number)
- account code
- budget period

In a large university, these identifiers consist of about 10 or 11 digits, with each digit encoding some aspect of the transaction.

The key to this code is the *chart of accounts*—a list of every account and fund in the accounting system along with its identifying number. Thus, when entering a transaction, a fiscal officer can look up the appropriate identifier in the chart of accounts. As the source of financial information that flows through the financial system, the chart of accounts is the organizing framework for all university financial transactions.

Most institutions use a chart-of-accounts numbering system based on the five account types. Typically, all asset accounts have a prefix of 1, while liability accounts have a prefix of 2, and so on. The numbering system looks like this, where the *x*'s are digits encoding other specific information:

- Assets: 1-xxxxxxxxxx
- Liabilities: 2-xxxxxxxxxx
- Net assets: 3-xxxxxxxxxx
- Revenues: 4-xxxxxxxxxx
- Expenses: 5-xxxxxxxxxx
- Other: 6-xxxxxxxxxx

This numbering system helps accountants keep track of accounts along with what category they belong to. For instance, if an account's name or description is ambiguous, the accountant can simply look at the prefix to know exactly what type it is. An asset would have the prefix of 1 and an expense would have a prefix of 5. This structure can avoid confusion in the accounting process and ensure the proper account is selected when recording transactions.

Fund Balances

In fund accounting, the term *fund balances* often replaces the term *net assets*. Consequently, the fundamental accounting equation is expressed in terms of fund balances instead of net assets. In equation form,

Assets = Liabilities + Fund Balances.

Like net assets, the fund balances depend on revenues and expenditures:

Fund Balances = Beginning Fund Balances + Revenues − Expenditures,

where the beginning fund balance refers to the cumulative fund balance at the time of the calculation. Accordingly, fund balances increase when revenues increase or expenditures decrease, and vice versa. If the beginning fund balance is zero, the fund balance simply equals the difference between revenues and expenditures. In practice, this difference (revenues minus expenditures) is the bottom line for each fund at the end of the fiscal year.

Conveniently, in fund accounting, money can be transferred from a positive balance in one fund to offset a negative balance in another fund. These transfers usually occur near the end of a fiscal year to balance the budget.

To calculate how much money a university has for discretionary use, one might reasonably expect to proceed by adding up the fund balances of all funds. After all, that is how most individuals would probably determine their discretionary net wealth: add up all of the liquid asset balances (bank accounts, stocks, and so forth) and subtract all of the liabilities (credit card bills, mortgages, car loans, and so forth). For a university, however, this approach does not work. Because some of the fund balances are restricted or administered by the university for a third party (such as a sorority or fraternity), the sum of all fund balances does not give a true measure of how much discretionary money a university has at its disposal. Indeed, the fund balance can be quite misleading, for an individual cannot easily tell from the financial documents whether funds are restricted or unrestricted and whether they are being spent properly.

To provide some clarity, fund balances are reported usually as reserved or unreserved.[9] When a fund balance is *reserved,* it can be spent only for a particular purpose. For instance, if grant monies from the federal government may be used only for research on kidney diseases, the fund balance would be reserved. When a fund balance is *unreserved*, it can be used for any purpose of the fund. For example, unreserved fund balances in the general fund can be used for any purpose at all. So, a sleuth looking for "hoarded" money should look first at unreserved fund balances.

Encumbrance Accounting

Encumbrance accounting is an important aspect of budgetary accounting in a university setting. By definition, an *encumbrance* is "a contingent liability, contract, purchase order, payroll commitment, tax payable, or legal penalty that is chargeable to an account. It ceases to be an encumbrance when paid-out or when the actual liability amount is determined and recorded as an expense."[10] Stated differently, an encumbrance is the name given to money that has been reserved to cover the cost of a purchase or payroll commitment.

Operationally, encumbrances are created in two steps. The first step occurs with the creation of a pre-encumbrance through the submission of a request for particular goods or services to the purchasing department. This request is known as a *purchase requisition* ("requisition" for short). If the purchasing department approves the requisition, the second step occurs when it submits a *purchase order* to a supplier for the goods or services. The purchase order creates the encumbrance.

When encumbrances are made (a purchase requisition is processed), funds are set aside to pay for that transaction when the invoice arrives. Those funds are no longer available for use in other transactions. Accordingly, when the encumbered expenditure is posted in the ledger, the amount of money required to fund the item is set aside in a temporary account as an obligation.

Liquidation refers to the paying of an encumbrance. When the vendor or employee is paid, the encumbrance is reversed—liquidated, in accounting terms—and the funds are recorded as an expenditure, thus reducing the fund balance. Occasionally, the amount billed differs from the amount encumbered, owing to unanticipated changes in price, tax, or freight charges. In those cases, the encumbrance must be corrected to account for the changes.

The purpose of encumbrance accounting is to avoid overspending. Outstanding (unliquidated) encumbrances are always subtracted from the actual fund balance to get a true picture of the funds available for future use. By recording the estimated cost of purchase orders and contracts as encumbrances, fiscal officers are aware of the future impact of a transaction. In practice, encumbrance accounting is invaluable for fund management.

Terminology Conventions

Finally, several terminology conventions used in this book should be noted. For simplicity, the term "university" will be used generically to refer to all institutions of higher education: two- and four-year colleges, regional universities, research universities, and so forth. Likewise, for simplicity, the term "college" will refer to all major academic units of a university, such as a college (for example, college of arts and sciences), a school (for example, medical school), and institute (for example, institute for advanced studies). The term "president" also will be used generically to refer to an institution's chief executive officer, regardless of the exact title: president, chancellor, rector. And the term "provost" will refer to the institution's chief academic officer. Moreover, it will be assumed that the provost is responsible for the academic operating budget. The term "chief budget officer" will refer to the individual responsible for the overall campus budget, who usually reports to the CFO.

Using the language of budgets and the terminology conventions introduced in this chapter, subsequent chapters will now explore university budgets in depth. The various types of university budgets will be examined, with a close look at how they are prepared and implemented.

Chapter 2

University Budgets

There is not just one university budget—there are many. In fact, budgets appear at every level of the university, often in different guises. At the department level, budgets manifest a performance agreement with the higher administration: stated simply, "give us money, and we will teach." At the campus level, they manifest a social contract, the culmination of a planning process: "with money, we will accomplish the university's mission." As seen in these two examples, the common feature that budgets manifest at all levels is money, making it easy to express priorities, expectations, and limitations quantitatively. Within this setting, this chapter takes a closer look at the different kinds of university budgets.

Budgets Defined

At the outset, it helps to know exactly what a budget is. The online Oxford Dictionary provides two simple definitions of a budget as a noun: "an estimate of income and expenditure for a set period of time" and "the amount of money needed or available for a purpose."[1] Thus, in its simplest form, a budget is an itemized list of estimated or intended expenditures for a given period of time along with estimated resources for financing them. Stated colloquially, the university's budget delineates who gets how much money for what. Accordingly, by this definition, a budget is a relatively straightforward document. For a given time period (such as a fiscal year), it tabulates items or services to be purchased and the proposed amount of money available to pay for these purchases—that is, the budgeted amount for each purpose. A budget can be as unpretentious as that: a list of things to buy and the amount of money available to pay for them. The simple definitions conform to the standard notion of a budget in most contexts, including households.

The Business Dictionary provides a more nuanced definition: "An estimate of costs, revenues, and resources over a specified period, reflecting a reading of future financial conditions and goals. One of the most important administrative tools, a budget serves also as a (1) plan of action for achieving quantified objectives, (2) standard for measuring performance, and (3) device for coping with foreseeable adverse situations."[2] This definition captures the more far-reaching significance of a budget in an academic setting. As this definition implies, the budget symbolizes the university's priorities, its goals. The list of things to buy represents items needed to accomplish the university's goals, and the money to pay for them represents the university's commitment to pursue these goals. According to this more nuanced definition, budgets bring income and expenditures into alignment with an institution's priorities.

The Oxford Dictionary provides a third definition of the word budget as a verb: "to provide (a sum of money) for a particular purpose from a budget."[3] For example, "we didn't budget for that" means that "we didn't anticipate that cost." Or, conversely, "we budgeted for that contingency" means that "we anticipated this cost." These last examples emphasize the impact of the budget as both a planning and an operational document.

Technically, these definitions do not imply that budgets represent transfers of university money. They represent transfers of authority to commit university money. Therefore, when a provost gives a college dean the college's budget, the provost gives the dean the authority to commit university money according to the budget. The provost has not made an expenditure; no money has changed hands. The dean may hire an employee, thus committing university money, but a fiscal officer spends the money (makes the expenditure) when issuing the employee's paycheck.

Because there are no standard guidelines for budget presentation, universities approach budgets in various ways. For example, some universities maintain separate budgets for each of their many funds. (The word "funds" is used in the fund-accounting context.) Alternatively, in a single budget, they may categorize revenues and expenditures according to fund type. Regardless, in practice, most budgets are prepared using accounting software that encodes fund accounting information. However, the detailed use of this information may not always be transparent outside the university budget offices. For pedagogical simplicity, the examples in this book will all assume a single fund.

Budgets are presented in two alternative formats: line-item and program. The *line-item budget* focuses on expenditures for specific goods and services. Characteristically, expenditures are listed according to their natural classification, with separate lines for salaries, supplies, travel, equipment, and so forth. This format shows which budget items absorb the bulk of the university's resources. Implicitly it limits the amount that can be spent on each line item, such as salaries, regardless of the perceived need. Most universities present their budgets in a line-item format.

Alternatively, universities may present their budgets in a *program format*, which focuses on specific programs. In this format, expenditures are listed according to their functional classification, with separate lines for instruction, research, public service, and so forth. This format provides a view of program effectiveness and efficiency, addressing the question: Is the budget aligned with the university's mission? Despite this advantage of the program format, it is used less commonly than the line-item format. As a best practice, budgets should be presented in both formats, since they provide complementary information about the university's performance.

On an institutional scale, universities usually have three major budget types: operating, capital, and auxiliary. Each has unique, distinguishing characteristics and plays a separate role on campus. Also, on a more restricted scale, universities have many small, project-specific budgets. Overall, the operating budget plays the central role, and the capital, auxiliary, and project-specific budgets play supporting roles.

Operating Budget

The institutional *operating budget* supports the primary mission of the university. It lists the revenues and expenditures necessary for the general operations of the university. Thus, it is of utmost interest to administrators and faculty members, for it relates to basic academic activities. How many faculty members can be hired this year? How many students can be given scholarships? How much money is available for new lab supplies?

Revenue for the operating budget comes from a variety of sources. They include tuition and fees, state appropriations, endowment income, grants and contracts, donors' gifts, and patent-generated income. The relative contributions from these various sources differ from one budget unit to the next. However, tuition and fees often constitute the major source of revenue. Revenue from tuition and fees is unrestricted; it can be used for any purpose. In contrast, revenue from grants and contracts and from some endowments and gifts is often restricted; it must be spent on specific programs or projects. Restrictions on revenue from state appropriations vary by state, ranging from totally unrestricted to highly restricted. Because of its flexibility, unrestricted income is preferred by administrators when preparing operating budgets.

Commonly, unrestricted revenue from the various sources that supports operations is transferred into a single fund, called the *general fund*. Stated another way, the general fund is used to account for all financial resources used to support operations except those that are required to be accounted for in another fund because of restrictions. Usually, universities have only one general fund. Consequently, the terms *operating budget* and *general fund budget* are often used interchangeably

Budget Hierarchy

Importantly, the institutional operating budget actually derives from a large variety of budget documents. Most organizational units in the academic hierarchy, ranging from the provost's office to the departments, have their own operating budget. This hierarchy is illustrated in figure 2.1. In this context, an organizational unit with an operating budget is known as a *budget unit*. Every department, school, college, center, administrative office, and service unit with its own operating budget is a budget unit. The head of each budget unit, the chairs, deans, directors, and so forth, are called budget unit directors. Within each budget unit, specific projects may have their own operating budgets. Every sponsored research grant, for example, has its own budget.

All of the budgets of the budget units in one level of the organizational hierarchy are merged into the operating budget of the next higher unit in the organizational hierarchy. So the departments' budgets are incorporated into the colleges' budgets, the colleges' budgets are incorporated into the provost's budget, and the provost's budget is consolidated into the institution's master operating budget. For that reason, the master budget is

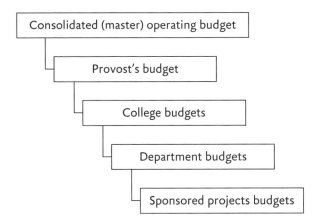

Figure 2.1. Operating budget hierarchy. Adapted from Dean O. Smith, *University Finances: Accounting and Budgeting Principles for Higher Education* (Baltimore, MD: Johns Hopkins University Press, 2019), p. 170.

called the *consolidated budget*. The university's chief budget officer, who reports to the CFO, oversees consolidation of the master budget.

This hierarchical structure of the operating budget offers programmatic advantages. It focuses attention on individual university programs, such as the academic departments and colleges. The alternative would be an operating budget for the entire institution, without regard to the individual programs. This kind of top-down budgeting generally would focus on cost containment rather than program effectiveness and efficiency. From an academic perspective, such a top-down approach is much less desirable than the hierarchical, bottoms-up approach.

But wait. A department chair might protest: "Department budgets are always top-down, since they come from the dean." Of course, that is true; they come from the dean, a higher level in the hierarchy. The point, however, is that the college budget derives from the department budgets. Potentially, this logic could engender an endless chicken-or-egg argument: Which comes first, the college or the departmental budget? This argument is best deferred until the process of preparing the budget has been explained further in chapter 5.

Nonetheless, department budgets will first be examined here from the department chair's perspective, as a document handed down from the dean. Then they will be followed as they move from the bottom up into the hierarchy.

Department Budgets

Department budgets constitute the foundational layer of the budget hierarchy. They guide expenditures within departments: salaries, supplies, travel, and other operational expenses. Therefore, the department budgets have the greatest impact on the routine activities of the department members.

The original operating budget at the start of each year is called the *base budget*. It represents the department's annual revenue allocation from the overall university operating budget. With rare exceptions, base budgets are balanced at the beginning of the year: the total authorized expenditures equal the revenue allocation.

In general, department budgets are prepared using standard templates generated by accounting software and issued by the chief budget officer. Nowadays, the templates are usually forms to be filled out online, with automatic calculations and internal edits to ensure compliance with university budget-office guidelines. Moreover, these templates contain the total revenue allocations to the departmental budget units, usually filled in by budget officers at the next-higher level in the academic hierarchy. In addition, they contain generic expenditure categories for salaries and operations. Some categories in these standard templates may not apply to particular budget units, so of course they are left blank. Typically, the previous year's actual revenues and expenditures are shown for comparison.

Department budgets contain various levels of detail, depending on the audience. For audiences outside the department, at a minimum they list expenditures in summary format, usually according to their natural classification (table 1.1). Often, they expand on this minimal summary format by listing various position types such as faculty, administrative, and graduate assistant. In the most detailed format, the budget lists every position, usually with the incumbent's name, title, percent appointment, base salary, fringe benefits, and salary source. This information may be in the budget document itself or a supplementary spreadsheet. Because of the sensitive nature of these salary details, the audience for this detailed budget is usually limited to the department chair, key administrative staff members, and, perhaps, several senior faculty members.

Salaries constitute the most frequent items in the department budget. Accordingly, the budget office typically pulls information for each approved position—employee's name, title, salary, appointment date, and so forth—from the human resources office's payroll records for each department and forwards this information to department administrators for inclusion in the budget. Usually, the department administrators, such as the department chair or budget officer, cannot alter these entries or access the raw budget files; only the issuing budget office has that authority. This security procedure prevents any unwarranted changes in an individual's salary or other appointment detail.

A sample departmental line-item operating budget in expanded summary format is illustrated in table 2.1. (For brevity, detailed position entries are not included.) Hypothetically, the department received the budget within a standard template generated by the accounting software from the dean's budget officer with expenditure categories and authorized spending amounts already filled in. Noticeably, some fields have been left blank (for example, Professional, Classified employee, Rent)

TABLE 2.1. *Department operating budget for 2020*

	2019 actual	2020 projected	Change Amount	%
Revenue allocation	980,000	1,000,000	20,000	2.04
Expenditures				
Salaries				
Faculty	670,000	700,000	30,000	4.48
Professional				
Administrative	112,000	100,000	(12,000)	−10.71
Classified employee				
Graduate assistant	40,000	40,000		
Faculty summer salary				
Student wages	8,000	8,000		
Other compensation	2,000	2,000		
Termination payouts				
Subtotal salaries	832,000	850,000	18,000	2.16
Operations				
Contracted services	15,000	12,000	(3,000)	−20.00
Supplies and materials	10,000	10,000		
Communications	4,000	4,000		
Travel	10,000	10,000		
Rent				
Utilities				
Repairs and maintenance	1,000	1,000		
Other	8,000	13,000	5,000	62.50
Subtotal operations	48,000	50,000	2,000	4.17
Scholarships	100,000	100,000		
Total expenditures	980,000	1,000,000	20,000	2.04

because they do not apply to this particular department. The 2020 base budget ("2020 projected") authorizes the department to spend $700,000 on faculty salaries, $12,000 on contracted services, and so forth for the remaining line items.

As shown in this example, most operating budgets throughout the hierarchy tabulate not only the current-year budget (2020) based on projected revenue and expenditures but also actual revenues and expenditures from the previous year (2019) for comparison. The change from the previous year's actual budget to the current year's projected budget is expressed as a dollar amount and a percentage. Calculation of the percentage change uses the following standard formula:

$$\% \text{ Change} = \frac{\text{Projected 2020 Budget} - \text{Actual 2019 Budget}}{\text{Actual 2019 Budget}} \times 100.$$

So, in this sample budget, the projected revenue allocation for 2020 ($1,000,000) increased by $20,000 relative to 2019 ($980,000), which is a 2.04 percent increase. Because the base budget is balanced (revenues equal expenditures) at the beginning of the fiscal year, the department's authorized expenditures also increased by 2.04 percent in 2020 relative to 2019.

Note that if the revenue allocation is simply a single number ($1,000,000 in this example), some department budget templates do not include a line item for revenue. By inference, the revenue allocation equals total expenditures. However, more complex department budget models with multiple revenue sources generally list specific revenue sources. They will be introduced in chapter 3.

Significantly, in this example, salaries make up 85 percent of the total operating budget expenditures ($850,000/$1,000,000), and faculty salaries make up 70 percent of the total budget. Many academic departments have salary percentages at least this high. In some departments, faculty salaries can exceed 95 percent of the total operating budget. Percentages this high leave little wiggle room when departments must accommodate budget cuts.

At some public universities, the department budgets do not include faculty salaries or fringe benefits, which are paid directly by some office higher in the hierarchy. For example, in Texas, the state pays faculty members' fringe benefits directly, so these fringe benefit expenditures do not appear in the departments' budgets. As a best practice, department chairs should nonetheless be aware of the actual costs covered by these other units or the state.

College Budgets

Moving up in the hierarchy, the department budgets are merged into the college budget. Stated the other way around, the college budget consists primarily of the combined budgets of all the budget units in the college. That includes the departments, centers and institutes, and any other academic service activities, plus, of course, the operational costs of the college itself.

College budgets usually list expenditures in a line-item format that aggregates proposed expenditures by budget units, such as departments. The total expenditures for each department (its bottom line) are listed on a separate line in the college budget. If the college has ten departments, then there are ten lines, one for each department, as well as a separate line for college operations. For some audiences, the college may add additional details to each line item. For example, it may add separate lines under each department line listing expenditures for salaries, supplies, travel, and so forth for that department. Like department budgets, the line-item format also shows the actual revenue and expenditures from the prior fiscal year for comparison.

Provost's Budget

In the next level up the hierarchy, the college budgets are merged into the provost's budget. Likewise, the budgets of all other academic support units are merged into the provost's budget. These include student affairs (enrollment management, the registrar), the graduate school, possibly sponsored research and intercollegiate athletics, and so forth. Thus, the provost's budget pertains to the university's core academic mission. The provost's budget is structured just like the college budgets. The line items consist of the various colleges and, in some cases, the departments itemized under their respective colleges.

Consolidated Budget

At the top of the hierarchy, the operating budgets for all major budget units are consolidated into the university's master operating budget. It includes the operating budgets from the provost, the CFO, the physical plant, the human resources office, the sponsored projects office, and so forth. Appropriately, this *master budget* is called the *consolidated budget*. It, too, is usually prepared in line-item format.

Because the consolidated budget contains so much information, most institutions generally prepare it in summary format for external audiences and the governing board, with one line for each major budget unit. At most, they sometimes break it down by major fund groups. For internal audiences, however, many institutions post the detailed budgets for every budget unit online. Because they include the names and salaries of specific personnel, access to these details is usually limited to a handful of senior administrators or, at most, current university employees. Individual sponsored grant and contract budget details are generally in a separate document that is available through the office of sponsored projects, although total grant and contract revenues and expenditures are usually summarized as a line in the consolidated budget.

A consolidated operating budget is illustrated in summary format in table 2.2. Unlike the sample department operating budget (table 2.1), the consolidated budget itemizes revenue sources. In this format, it is easy to see that state appropriations constitute more than half of the revenue. Moreover, they rose by $3,000,000, or 6.25 percent, for 2020. Also, it compresses the eight operations expenditures itemized in the department budget (table 2.1) into a single line item for brevity. In total, the 2020

TABLE 2.2. *Consolidated operating budget for 2020*

	2019 actual	2020 projected	Change Amount	%
Revenues				
Tuition	19,000,000	20,000,000	1,000,000	5.26
Student fees	450,000	500,000	50,000	11.11
State appropriations	48,000,000	51,000,000	3,000,000	6.25
Grants and contracts	6,800,000	7,000,000	200,000	2.94
Auxiliary	10,000,000	11,000,000	1,000,000	10.00
Outreach	1,250,000	1,400,000	150,000	12.00
Total	85,500,000	90,900,000	5,400,000	6.32
Expenditures				
Salaries and wages	60,000,000	63,000,000	3,000,000	5.00
Fringe benefits	18,000,000	21,000,000	3,000,000	16.67
Operations	5,000,000	4,900,000	(100,000)	−2.00
Scholarships	2,000,000	2,000,000		
Total	85,000,000	90,900,000	5,900,000	6.94
Fund balance	500,000		(500,000)	−100.00

projected expenditures increase by $5,900,000, which is 6.94 percent more than the actual expenditures in 2019.

In this example, the 2019 revenues exceeded expenditures by $500,000, resulting in a $500,000 fund balance. That savings could be rolled forward into the 2020 budget or transferred to another account for some purpose not listed in the budget (for example, deferred maintenance). In this example, it was transferred to another account, thus zeroing the beginning fund balance for 2020. At the outset, the 2020 budget is balanced; revenues equal expenditures, for a zero fund balance. By the end of the year, the actual revenues and expenditures most probably will not be equal (as in 2019), resulting in a positive or negative fund balance.

Because of the operating budget's importance and interest to the academic community, its preparation, implementation, and closing will be examined much more closely in chapters 3 through 7. First, however, the other university budget types warrant introductory attention: capital, auxiliary, and project-specific budgets.

Capital Budget

The capital budget is a plan for spending large sums of money for investment in property, plant, and equipment: projects that will have ongoing effects on the institution's operations, such as buildings, renovations, roads, and major equipment items. Stated more simply, the capital budget is a spending plan for capital assets. Most institutions limit inclusion in the capital budget to proposed capital-asset expenses greater than a threshold value of, say, $100,000. Any project costing less than that threshold is included in the operating budget (for example, in the "Other" line item in table 2.1). Unlike an operating budget, which pertains to a single fiscal year, the capital budget extends for several years, the time span for planning, design, and construction of a new building or for scheduled major maintenance or infrastructure projects.

Revenue sources for the capital budget include cash from the general fund, reserves, state and federal appropriations, gifts from donors, and endowment income. Commonly, however, universities borrow money to pay for them; they incur debt. In the business vernacular, when a university borrows money to be paid back at a future date with interest, it is using *debt financing.* Even when a donor pledges money for a new building, universities often use debt financing: they borrow money to pay for the building up front and use the donation proceeds to make the periodic interest plus principal payments over the duration of the long-term debt.

When borrowing money for capital assets, universities often issue bonds, a form of long-term debt. A bond issue is generally less expensive than borrowing money from a bank and is subject to fewer restrictive covenants—rules placed on debt to reduce the lender's risk. When issuing bonds, universities must identify where the money to repay the debt will come from. There are two primary sources: money from revenue generated by tuition and fees and other sources contributing to the operating budget or money from the revenue stream generated by the capital asset, such as dormitory or dining hall fees. In both cases, the bonds are known as *revenue bonds*.

To minimize the cost of borrowing money, universities often take advantage of an Internal Revenue Service (IRS) provision that allows state and local governments to issue tax-exempt bonds on behalf of both public and private universities.[4] More exactly, the interest paid to the bond purchasers, the bondholders, is tax-exempt; the bondholder does not have to pay federal taxes on the interest income. Moreover, most states do not tax the interest income from tax-exempt bonds issued within that state (virtually all states, however, tax the interest from tax-exempt bonds issued in another state). Because of these tax advantages, bondholders accept a lower rate of interest, thus reducing the amount of interest that universities must pay the bondholders.

Sometimes, an institution needs financing for a capital asset but cannot issue long-term debt because of state-mandated debt ceilings, for example. Or it wants to circumvent certain bond limitations. In these cases, the institution may structure financing in a way that is not considered debt under state law, such as lease-backed financing. In this method, called *lease financing* for short, instead of buying a capital asset with bond proceeds, the institution (the lessee) leases the capital asset from the lessor (usually the owner of the asset), with lease payments coming from the institution's operating budget. In a *lease-purchase agreement*, the lease payments apply toward the purchase price of the asset; at the end of the lease, the institution owns the asset. Leases are not considered debt because the institution can theoretically stop making lease payments at any time—it can just walk away, relinquishing the asset. Of course, this seldom happens, because it would likely face significant financial penalties.

This alternative method of acquiring a capital asset often involves issuance of so-called *certificates of participation* (COPs). In COP financing, the institution enters into a lease or lease-purchase agreement for a proposed facility owned by another party. For example, the facility may be an existing building or a new building constructed according to the institution's specifications. Typically, the agreement is between the institution and a trustee, such as a commercial bank. The trustee agrees to buy the facility from the owner and then lease it to the institution, which makes regular lease payments to the trustee. To generate money to pay for this purchase of the facility, the trustee issues COPs that entitle the investors who bought them to receive a participation, or share, of the lease payments made by the institution to the trustee. The term of the COPs equals the term of the lease. In other words, the principal received by the trustee from the purchasers of the COPs is used to buy the facility from the owner, thus transferring ownership to the trustee for the term of the lease. The trustee collects lease payments from the institution and makes payments to the investors. Note that it is not necessary for the trustee to be a nonprofit organization. Like bonds, COPs issued by universities can be tax-exempt. However, because they are inherently riskier than bonds, COPs have a lower credit rating than bonds and therefore pay higher interest rates.

Capital budgets are prepared typically by the CFO in consultation with the president, provost, and other senior members of the administration. Various constituencies recommend items for inclusion in the budget. For example, the provost might recommend specific new buildings and renovations to meet academic demands for space; the physical plant director might recommend specific upgrades to heating, ventilation, and air-conditioning systems to meet modern efficiency standards. As part of the capital budget process, the facilities office staff must also determine the nature and seriousness of any capital asset deficiencies, such as repairs that must be made. To keep track of each capital asset's condition, they maintain a capital asset condition inventory by routinely inspecting each capital asset on a regular basis—once every three years, for example. For most routine projects, cost estimates for repairing deficiencies are readily available from commercial data sources. The capital budget is nearly always subject to approval by the university's governing board, mainly because of the large amounts of money involved.

In practice, state legislatures often exert de facto control of public institutions' capital budgets through the appropriations process. The governor may also exert some level of control. Together or separately, they can determine whether state funding will be available for specific projects put forth by the university. Their political influence may be indirect. For example, a state-wide higher-education coordinating body (appointed by the governor) may reorder the university's list of priorities before it gets to the governor for submission to the legislature. Or their political influence may be direct. For example, the legislature or governor may express interest in a specific project that was not a priority for the university, resulting in funding specifically for the "pet" project rather than the university's top priority. Although most legislatures honor capital-project priorities submitted by the university administration, it is not unusual for political considerations to influence the actual appropriations.

In the capital budget, projects are typically listed in order of priority. The highest-priority project is the next to be undertaken and so on down the list. Every year or so, the list is revised, with some projects coming off or moving onto the list while others move up or down in priority. These revisions depend on funding availability, programmatic changes, and political considerations. Only a few top-ranked items are actually approved for funding in each year's capital budget. Some items lower on this list may never reach the top. However, a major donation for the construction of a specific new building can usually move that building quickly up in priority.

The priority of specific repairs on the capital budget list depends on the nature of the deficiencies. Their usual order of priority is as follows:

- health and safety issues
- building code violations
- damage or wear out
- environmental improvements
- energy conservation
- aesthetics
- building enhancements

Repairs affecting health and safety issues nearly always take top priority.

The skeletal elements of a capital budget are illustrated in table 2.3. In this table, which was prepared for FY 2020, various capital asset projects ranging from fire and safety upgrades to new construction are listed in priority along with their planned funding sources and estimated costs. For example, the top priority is the campus fire and safety upgrade. The second priority is the dormitory electrical system, which is in violation of code. And so on down the list.

The capital budget and operating budget are interrelated. As shown in table 2.3, the capital budget does not include the recurring costs of routine building operations and maintenance and of debt financing (for example, interest payments). Instead, the operating budget includes those costs. In this way, the capital budget impacts the operating budget. These routine costs can

TABLE 2.3. *Capital budget for 2020*

Priority	Project	Funding source	Expenditures			
			Total amount	Prior to 2020 actual	2020 projected	2021 and beyond projected
1	Campus fire and safety upgrade	General fund reserves	3,000,000	1,000,000	2,000,000	
2	Dormitory electrical code upgrade	Program revenue bonds	6,000,000	2,000,000	2,000,000	2,000,000
3	Campus utilities upgrade	Certificates of participation	1,600,000		600,000	1,000,000
4	Law library renovation	Donor gift and general fund	4,000,000		2,000,000	2,000,000
5	New addition to science building	General fund revenue bonds	30,000,000	10,000,000	10,000,000	10,000,000
6	New dormitory stage 1 design	Program revenue bonds	400,000		400,000	
	Total		45,000,000	13,000,000	17,000,000	15,000,000

be substantial, and they must always be taken into account when proposing a new building. For example, the annual interest payments on a $25 million bond issue (at a rate of 5 percent for 30 years) is about $1.6 million, and the annual operations and maintenance costs for a 100,000 square-foot building can be in the $600,000 range.[5] Those costs must be paid out of the operating budget, potentially at the expense of other academic programs. To ensure that a university can afford to pay them without adversely affecting the university's academic programs, many governing boards and states require an analysis of these recurring costs and a plan for paying them as part of a capital budget request for a new building.

In times of budgetary stress, institutions may defer costly maintenance: put off replacing an aging ventilation system, delay replacing a roof, and so forth. This results in so-called *deferred maintenance*. Deferred maintenance refers to building system deficiencies that affect the long-term renewal costs of the building—big-ticket items. It does not refer to relatively minor repairs covered by routine work orders. Left unchecked, deferred maintenance can erode campus facilities, with insidious consequences for teaching effectiveness and research capacity. Indeed, deferred maintenance costs are a lurking menace to a university's academic and financial well-being.

Capital budgets, therefore, often include deferred maintenance items, but they may not be identified explicitly as deferred maintenance. In table 2.3, for example, any of the first four projects could include deferred maintenance issues. By placing them in the capital budget, universities can spread the repair costs over several years.

Auxiliary Budgets

An auxiliary budget is developed for an *auxiliary enterprise*—that is, an operation that directly or indirectly supports the academic vision and mission of the university by providing a service to students, faculty, staff, or the general public and charges a fee for these services. Most institutions have separate auxiliary budgets for auxiliary activities such as residence facilities (dormitories and dining halls), hospitals, clinical practice plans, intercollegiate athletic programs, and specialized research centers. Auxiliary budgets are developed and controlled by directors, such as the hospital director, the center directors, and the athletic director. Furthermore, auxiliary enterprises may have their own advisory board, which must approve the fee structure and budget.

The most distinguishing characteristic of an auxiliary enterprise is that it must be managed as a self-supporting activity, and this feature is manifest in its budget. As a self-supporting activity, an auxiliary enterprise typically sets fees to match expenses—to break even. So revenue generated by the service, such as dormitory room and board fees, hospital fees, and athletic-event ticket income, generally equals expenditures. Furthermore, some universities allow auxiliary enterprises, as self-supporting activities, to keep the interest income gained from the investment of their excess cash. Thus, in principle, an auxiliary's budget is straightforward, with user fees matching expenses.

In practice, however, revenue and expenses do not always match. Some services may require subsidies, called *subvention* in academic jargon, if fees prove inadequate to meet expenses. For example, a university press may occasionally require subvention from the operating budget to offset a revenue shortfall. In those cases, the subvention is often treated like a loan, to be repaid to the university's operating budget. Moreover, some auxiliary enterprises, such as specific athletic programs, depend on donated revenue from groups like booster clubs to supplement fees to meet expenses. In other cases, revenue may flow in the opposite direction, from an auxiliary enterprise to the university's operating budget. The most notable example is a highly successful football program that generates income exceeding its budgetary needs, resulting in a fund balance that can be transferred into the operating budget. More commonly, successful university bookstores and continuing education programs may transfer a fund balance into the operating revenue.

Because they are self-supporting, auxiliary enterprises often establish reserve funds to pay for maintenance and repair expenses or cyclical expenses when the need arises. Money designated for the reserve funds is commonly built into the fee structure. The transfer of money into a reserve fund is recorded as an expenditure in the budget.

A sample budget for an auxiliary enterprise, intercollegiate athletics, is shown in table 2.4. In this example, expenditures are listed only according to natural classification. Customarily, these budgets also list expenditures by functional classification as an integral part of the budget or as a supplementary spreadsheet. For athletics, the functional line items are usually by team: football, women's basketball, men's basketball, and so on. In either classification, the line items are noticeably different from the generic academic operating budget. This difference reflects the more specialized nature of the auxiliary enterprise.

This example illustrates transfers of money from one fund to another within the institution. They include transfers of $250,000 and $200,000 to campus-wide deferred maintenance and plant debt service funds. These transfers represent the intercollegiate athletics program's proportional share of the overall costs of maintenance, acquisition, and renovation of campus facilities.

This example also illustrates campus subvention to balance the budget. In 2019, actual expenditures exceeded revenue by $1,000,000; the program ended the year in the hole. To balance its year-end 2019 budget, the intercollegiate athletic program borrowed $1,000,000 from the provost, with the understanding that the program would repay the loan in equal payments of $200,000

	2019 actual	2020 projected	Change	
			Amount	%
Revenue				
Spectator admissions	3,500,000	3,800,000	300,000	8.57
Conference distributions	1,000,000	1,200,000	200,000	20.00
Gifts	1,230,000	1,340,000	110,000	8.94
Corporate sponsorship	100,000	100,000		
Licensing royalties	50,000	50,000		
Facility revenues	22,000	18,000	(4,000)	−18.18
Concessions and parking	8,000	7,000	(1,000)	−12.50
Other	3,000	3,000		
Subtotal operating revenue	5,913,000	6,518,000	605,000	10.23
Subvention	1,000,000		(1,000,000)	−100.00
Total revenue	6,913,000	6,518,000	(395,000)	−5.71
Expenditures				
Salaries, wages, and benefits	2,300,000	2,000,000	(300,000)	−13.04
Financial aid to students	2,000,000	2,000,000		
Team and game expenses	1,500,000	1,300,000	(200,000)	−13.33
Other operating expenses	600,000	500,000	(100,000)	−16.67
Transfer to university		200,000	200,000	
Facility expenses	63,000	68,000	5,000	7.94
Deferred maintenance fund transfer	250,000	250,000		
Plant debt service fund transfer	200,000	200,000		
Total expenditures	6,913,000	6,518,000	(395,000)	−5.71

for each of the next five years. The loan is recorded as a subvention in 2019. The first repayment is recorded as a "transfer to university" expenditure in 2020. To balance the projected 2020 budget and offset the need for further subvention, the intercollegiate athletics program increased revenue by raising ticket prices ("spectator admissions") by 8.57 percent and reducing expenditures for operating costs (salaries, wages, benefits, etc.) by 5.71 percent.

Project-Specific Budgets

The most abundant budgets within a university are for specific projects. The projects range from large research grants to small travel grants to attend a professional conference. In each case, the budget allocates revenue and authorizes expenditure of university funds.

Grant applications to organizations external to the university almost always include a project-specific budget. Most granting organizations, including federal agencies such as the National Science Foundation and the National Institutes of Health, provide budget templates that document what can and cannot be included in the budget. Moreover, they may revise the budget before making an award. Grant budgets award money to the university, which then authorizes the principal investigator to commit for specific items listed in the award. Implicitly, these expenditures must be related to the specific project. Explicitly, expenditures using federal funds must be spent according to guidelines established by the Office of Management and Budget's (OMB) *Uniform Administrative Requirements, Cost Principles, and Audit Requirements for Federal Awards*, commonly called the *Uniform Guidance*.[6] Most universities have an office of sponsored projects that oversees compliance with these guidelines.

Within the university, project-specific budgets arise routinely at all levels of the hierarchy. Basically, they pertain to individual projects that fall within the umbrella of normal operations. For example, when a faculty member asks the department chair for funds to pay for the cost of attending a professional conference (travel, lodging, meals, and registration fees), a common answer is, "Okay, but bring me a budget." So the faculty member prepares a simple budget, itemizing the projected expenditures:

taxi fares, air fare, per diem for lodging and meals, and so forth. Revenue for this travel budget comes from the department's resources, such as the operating budget or an endowment fund. By approving the budget, the department chair formally authorizes the faculty member to commit university funds. Of course, the authorization is limited to the amount approved by the chair in the budget. In that way, the chair controls the expenditures, because implicitly the faculty member is not authorized to spend more than the budgeted amount. There are many other imaginable scenarios involving these relatively small project-specific budgets.

Usually, these small project-specific budgets are not recorded formally per se, but the expenditures are recorded as a component of the overall department operating budget or other fund budget, such as an endowment or gift fund.

Position Budgets

Like most organizations, universities keep track of their workforce by a process known as *position control*. The budget and human resources offices typically control this function by assigning a number to each authorized position. Aptly, this is known as the *position number*. The positions and their numbers have several other names, such as slots and billets.

Because specific employees come and go, each position in the workforce is tracked independently from the employee who occupies that position. Position control creates a framework of positions for all the jobs within the university regardless of whether there is an incumbent in a specific job. Significantly, position control applies to all regular faculty, staff, and student employment positions but not to independent contractors and consultants.

As a corollary to position control, budgets refer technically to positions, not to individual employees. Accordingly, each position has a *position budget* that authorizes the specific amount of money available to fund that specific position, not specific individuals who are in the position. Conceptually, this is known as position budgeting.

The link between position number and position budget provides control over the hiring process. An individual cannot be hired into a position that does not have a number. As a result, an individual is hired into either an existing vacant position that already has a number or a newly created position that has been assigned a number. Colloquially, because one cannot exist without the other, the terms position and position number are used interchangeably.

Usually, requests for a new position number include workload justifications, job descriptions, minimum and desired qualifications, suggested pay range, funding sources, and similar information. Generally, the office of human resources must review these requests to ensure consistency with university employment guidelines. The requests require the approval of supervisors up the hierarchy; for example, a dean must approve a new department position and the provost must approve a new college-level position. Ultimately, the new position must be approved by the CFO—or in some institutions, the president—before the chief budget officer issues the position number and places it into the budget.

Ideologically, the purpose of this extensive approval process is to ensure that the new position conforms to the strategic plan and that a budget unit does not stray outside its prescribed boundaries of operation or engage in mission creep. Furthermore, this process allows any of the higher-level reviewers (for example, deans or provost) to intervene at a critical point if they want to force an increase in the budget unit's productivity or quality of service by adjusting the generosity of their position number assignments.

Pragmatically, position control enables tracking of position vacancies, staffing needs, and salary budgeting, while it prevents overhiring and budget deficiencies. Moreover, it provides information about the total cost of salary and benefits for each employee, indicating whether the position is fully funded and the source of funding. Consequently, position control is an important aspect of budget preparation and implementation.

Managing position control has become fairly simple with the use of modern software systems, such as PeopleSoft and Banner, which have position control modules. They will not allow the hiring process to begin without an appropriate position number. Nor will they allow a unit to hire an employee at a salary higher than the amount approved in the budget.

In some universities, position control is based on numerical metrics, such as student enrollment per major or student-to-faculty ratio. Therefore, on the one hand, if a department's student-to-faculty ratio increases above a targeted value owing to increased enrollment or unfilled position vacancies, the salary budget increases commensurate with the number of positions needed to restore the ratio to its desired value. On the other hand, without the necessary position numbers, the mere availability of money does not permit a department to hire new faculty members to lower the student-to-faculty ratio.

States commonly use position-control metrics like enrollment when allocating funds to their public universities. Indeed, procedurally, they allocate positions and then the funds to pay for these positions. By limiting the number of allocated positions, states effectively impose position control. Private university governing boards also may limit the number of allocable positions, thus limiting the size of the budget. In this sense, the universities, public and private, are budgeting people.

The importance and managerial convenience of position control and position budgets are illustrated further by a counterexample. If budgets were person oriented (not position oriented), they would be based on current-year payroll activity. If a vacancy in a position carried over into the next fiscal year, money for the vacant position would disappear from the next year's budget because a person was no longer being paid through the payroll system. At that point, vacant positions would exist solely in the recollection of the hiring manager and a personnel file in human resources. As Michelle Aloia, director of financial planning and analysis at Saint Xavier University, points out in her essay on position control, eventually time and personnel turnover would erode knowledge about vacancies and their funding sources, resulting in a "perpetual misunderstanding" of which positions were approved for inclusion in the budget "since static details of the budget did not exist."[7] With this misunderstanding, the validity of the budget would come into question.

Budget Uncertainties

Budgets harbor uncertainties. This occurs mainly because budgets by definition are planning documents that project into the future. They depend on inherently imprecise estimates of enrollment, personnel changes, inflation, state tax revenue, ticket sales, and other financial variables. Changes in any of these parameters can alter a budget, sometimes quite significantly. Moreover, universities usually are not obligated to spend money in precise accordance with their budget, which is merely a planning document. For example, a budget may allocate a certain amount of salary for faculty positions. However, in any given year some faculty members leave the institution for one reason or another. If the position is not filled immediately, some percentage of the budgeted faculty salaries usually is either re-budgeted to some other item or accumulated in the fund balance, becoming part of the university's financial reserves. Therefore, the budgeted amount for faculty salaries is not necessarily the actual amount spent on salaries.

Despite these uncertainties, budgets play a central role in all aspects of a university's activities. Indeed, they establish both financial and programmatic guidelines for all academic and auxiliary operations. To affirm this assertion, the following chapters will explore the preparation and implementation of these crucial documents. Initially, the next chapter will examine variations on the basic operating budget model introduced in this chapter.

Chapter 3

Budget Models

U niversity budgets are based on models. In this context, the term "model" refers to "a simplified description, especially a mathematical one, of a system or process, to assist calculations and predictions."[1] A *budget model* is thus a simplified description of the process used to construct a budget. This concept can be extended more specifically: because revenue drives the budget, the budget model describes the process used to allocate revenue. In practice, universities allocate revenue at each level in the hierarchy according to their budget models. This chapter explores this fundamental budget concept in further detail.

Revenue Allocation Basis

Revenue allocation is the keystone to the operating budget. This is the point when department aspirations meet financial reality. It is the point when the provost has the opportunity to reallocate funds, rewarding well-performing or particularly high-priority units; when institutions can implement changes in programmatic direction; and when the provost decides how much revenue to keep in reserve for unexpected situations, a common practice known as *underallocation*. (Note that the same could be said about the dean when allocating revenue to the departments. For brevity, most of this chapter will focus on the provost, but the principles apply to the dean as well.)

Seldom does a provost decide on revenue allocations on a whim. More often than not, the institution has adopted formal guidelines for making these decisions. These guidelines are usually based on some model for budget allocations. Within academia, there are four standard budget allocation models:

- zero-based
- incremental
- formula-based
- revenue-based

The principles of each model will be discussed. It should be noted beforehand, though, that in practice the allocation procedures may not follow any model precisely; a university may follow a hybrid procedure that reflects overlapping procedures from two or three of these models.

Incidentally, revenue from student fees usually is not included in these revenue-allocation algorithms. It is returned to the programs that generated it. If the chemistry department charges a $50 glass-breakage fee for each student enrolled in a chemistry course, the department keeps that money.

Zero-Based Budgeting

In *zero-based budgeting*, the harshest, most centralized budget model, each unit must justify from the ground up all of its proposed expenditures. This is tantamount to justifying its very existence every fiscal year. On the one hand, this allocation model is responsive to current performance and needs. On the other hand, it seriously hampers long-range planning. In principle, therefore, tenure guarantees a job but not a salary. Plus, in zero-based budget models, budget hearings expand into full-scale performance reviews, which consume considerable time and effort on the part of both the administration and the faculty members. Consequently, academic institutions seldom adhere to a zero-based budget model. At most, they may reduce the base relative to the previous year by a more manageable amount, such as 10 or 15 percent, and require justifications for increasing expenditures relative to that reduced base. (Of course, in that case the budget is no longer zero-based.)

Incremental Budgeting

In the widely used *incremental budgeting* model, funding increments are added to (or subtracted from) the previous year's budget. Procedurally, the prior year's budget is rolled over into the next fiscal year, becoming the base. Then, the current year's incremental adjustments are made to the line items in this base. In this way, the next year's budget depends on the previous year's budget, following historical trends. The underlying assumption is that the institution's fundamental goals and objectives do not change markedly from this year to the next.

An across-the-board incremental budgeting model is the easiest to implement. The provost or dean simply adds or subtracts a percentage increment from each unit's previous year's budget. The incremental amount depends on the overall amount of revenue available to the institution. If the university's state appropriations increase by 2 percent, each budget unit's allocation increases by 2 percent, less any amount withheld by the CFO, provost, or dean for special purposes. A common example of incremental budgeting occurs if the state or the governing board includes a 2 percent increase in the budget specifically to fund salary increases. The 2 percent incremental allocation is simply added to each unit's budget. Department chairs may have the discretion to base an individual's salary raise on performance metrics, budget hearings, committee recommendations, and other criteria. In that case, the overall incremental amount available for pay raises is constant (2 percent), but not all individuals necessarily get equal incremental raises.

Selective incremental changes for specific line items are somewhat more difficult to implement. Typically, department chairs and deans request incremental increases in the budgeted amounts for specific line items, or, when budgets are being reduced, they ask to exclude specific line items from the reductions. Then, the deans and the provost, respectively, must decide which requests to approve. For college budgets, the provost may allow the deans the opportunity to justify their requests in budget hearings and committee reviews, whereas for department budgets, the dean is more likely to decide on increments to the base with less formal consultation. At both levels, the decision-making process often devolves into a negotiation process. For this reason, this model is known cynically as the "history and mystery" budget model.

A simple example of an incremental budget request by a department is shown in table 3.1. The budget template (derived from table 2.1) came electronically to the department with standard expenditure categories and budget numbers for 2019 filled in by the accounting software. The department's budget request for the next year, 2020, is expressed as increments to the base, the prior year's (2019) budget. The department's budget officer entered the incremental amounts requested in next year's budget ("2020 increment") into the boxes; these entries are shown in italics. The software automatically calculated the percentage change of the totals requested for 2020 relative to the 2019 base. Overall, the department is requesting a 10.00 percent ($100,000) incremental increase in the 2020 budget. The requested 2020 budget is then submitted electronically to the dean's office for consideration.

Noticeably, the revenue allocation is not shown on the template. In this simple incremental budget request, the department has no idea what sources contributed to its revenue allocation.

TABLE 3.1. *Department incremental budget request for 2020*

Expenditures	2019 base	2020 increment Amount	%	2020 requested
Salaries				
Faculty	700,000	*50,000*	7.14	750,000
Professional				
Administrative	100,000			100,000
Classified employee				
Graduate assistant	40,000	*20,000*	50.00	60,000
Faculty summer salary				
Student wages	8,000			8,000
Other compensation	2,000			2,000
Termination payouts				
Subtotal salaries	850,000	70,000	8.24	920,000
Operations				
Contracted services	12,000	*3,000*	25.00	15,000
Supplies and materials	10,000	*2,000*	20.00	12,000
Communications	4,000			4,000
Travel	10,000			10,000
Rent				
Utilities				
Repairs and maintenance	1,000			1,000
Other	13,000			13,000
Subtotal operations	50,000	5,000	10.00	55,000
Scholarships	100,000	*25,000*		125,000
Total expenditures	1,000,000	100,000	10.00	1,100,000

Note: Italic data in the boxes were filled in by the department, and all other data were entered automatically by the accounting software.

All it knows is that the revenue comes from one source, an allocation from the dean. Conceivably, the dean may not know what sources contributed to the college's budget; the revenue just came from the provost with no explanation. For the 2019 base budget in this example, the revenue allocation presumably equaled the authorized total expenditures ($1,000,000). For 2020, the revenue allocation will depend on the amount of the increments approved by the dean. At most, the inferred revenue will be $1,100,000.

Incremental budgeting has advantages and disadvantages. On the one hand, its simplicity reduces the administrative burden of extensive budget hearings and consultations. A budget unit's continued existence is not at stake. Also, its stability eases long-range planning; although the exact magnitude of future increments may be unknown, at least the budget units know that they will not be singled out for hugely disproportional budget cuts because of decreased performance or enrollment. On the other hand, incremental budgeting lacks incentives. This is the serious downside to its stability; budget units are not rewarded for exceptional performance. For this reason, a budget unit's enthusiasm for incremental budgeting depends on its expected performance. Furthermore, incremental budgeting maintains a department's or college's relative share of the total revenue available, with little regard for changes in teaching load or sponsored research activity. In a sense, prior-year base budgets become entitlements, with past expenditures, not revenue, guiding budget preparation.

Ironically, the line item format confers a dubious advantage. It simplifies rolling forward the budget into a new year. However, this simplicity poses a significant disadvantage if it discourages careful analysis of the budget units' past performance, thus perpetuating past expenditure outlays into the future. As a best practice, college deans should always resist the temptation simply to roll forward the budget without careful analysis.

Formula-Based Budgeting

Formula-based budget models allocate revenue according to selected productivity metrics. The formulas vary in complexity, but most predicate the allocations on several standard metrics.

Semester credit hours, number of full-time-equivalent students, or total number of students are the most prevalent bases in the instruction, academic support, and institutional support areas. Square footage is the base used most often in the operation and maintenance of the physical plant, and total student enrollment ("headcount") is the base used most often in student services and financial aid. Thus, in the simplest formula, instructional allocations might depend on a college's enrollment, such as $100 per student. Or they might depend on the number of semester credit hours taught; for example, a college teaching 10 percent of the credit hours would receive 10 percent of the overall instructional budget. Formulas may also be based on specific performance measures, such as increased retention and graduation rates, reductions in time to degree, number of grant applications submitted, and number of papers published.

The metrics—such as semester credit hours or square footage—measured at a specific time, such as the end of the fall semester, are commonly averaged over a three-year period to smooth out any unusual fluctuations. For example, if a college taught 800, 1,000, and 1,200 semester credit hours in the fall semester of fiscal years 2017, 2018, and 2019, respectively, the three-year average is 1,000 semester credit hours. This number is then multiplied by a base rate to attain the allocation. If the base rate is $50 per semester credit hour, the college would receive an allocation of $50,000 ($1,000 × $50) in the FY 2020 budget. Notably, the base rate depends on the projected revenue; if the projected revenue available for budgeting increases or decreases, then the base rate increases or decreases, respectively.

Formulas become more complicated if they add a weighting scheme to account for differences between student levels (freshman, sophomore, graduate, and so forth) and academic disciplines (liberal arts, engineering, business, and so forth). Usually, the relative weights account for differential costs of delivering instruction. For example, if the least expensive cost of instruction is for undergraduates in the liberal arts, this category is assigned a baseline weight of 1. If the cost of undergraduate instruction in the college of engineering is three times more expensive, the college of engineering is assigned a weight of 3 in the allocation formula. Therefore, for each semester credit hour taught, the college of engineering would be allocated three times as much revenue as the college of liberal arts. In practice, weighting schemes generally introduce accounting complications. Nonetheless, institutions that use a formula-based model for revenue allocations tend to adopt a more-or-less complicated weighting scheme.

Practical usage of the weighting algorithm for three different colleges (business, engineering, and arts and sciences) within a university is illustrated in table 3.2. Initially, a matrix of weights is prepared, and the semester credit hours are tabulated. As in most cases, the semester credit hours represent the average of the fall semester data for the preceding three years to smooth out large fluctuations. The semester credit hour values are multiplied by the corresponding relative weights to attain the weighted semester credit hours. Finally, the weighted semester credit hours are multiplied by the base rate to calculate the allocated revenue for each college. So, in the college of arts and sciences, the 20,000 semester credit hours taught to undergraduates generate $1 million in revenue for the college's budget ($1 \times 20{,}000 \times \$50$). In addition, the 2,000 semester credit hours taught to graduate students generate 10,000 weighted semester credit hours and, therefore, $500,000 in revenue for the college's budget ($5 \times 2{,}000 \times \$50$).

Using a comparable methodology, utilities and operations and maintenance budget allocations can be calculated. Weights may be applied, depending on the building's use: energy-hungry laboratories and computing facilities may be assigned higher weights. The square footage for each building is multiplied by the appropriate weight en route to the final allocation.

Some units are not suitable for formula-based allocations. Central administration activities, for example, seldom have

TABLE 3.2. *Formula funding based on weighted semester credit hours*

College	Undergraduate	Graduate	Total
Weights			
Business	2	4	
Engineering	3	6	
Arts and sciences	1	5	
Semester credit hours			
Business	3,000	1,000	
Engineering	2,000	3,000	
Arts and sciences	20,000	2,000	
Weighted semester credit hours			
Business	6,000	4,000	
Engineering	6,000	18,000	
Arts and sciences	20,000	10,000	
Base rate ($ per weighted semester credit hour) = $50			
Allocations ($)			
Business	300,000	200,000	500,000
Engineering	300,000	900,000	1,200,000
Arts and sciences	1,000,000	500,000	1,500,000
Total	1,600,000	1,600,000	3,200,000

Note: Allocations equal the base rate times the weighted semester credit hours.

quantifiable activities. Consequently, they may not be included in the formula-based allocation process. Instead, they may be funded separately by an incremental process, which decreases the funds available for distribution according to the formula. Although reducing the fraction of resources allocated through the formula in this way is unavoidable, the reductions weaken incentives and impede reallocations needed to meet demand.

A majority of states use a formula-based process for allocating appropriations to the public institutions of higher education. At the state level, the weighting schemes can become quite detailed, for the weights reflect the myriad educational, political, economic, and public policy factors that influence the financing of higher education. Texas, for example, uses a complicated algorithm, with more than one hundred different weights in the instructional allocation formula.[2] In fiscal year 2019, the base rate was $55.82. Thus, an institution received $55.82 for every semester credit hour taught to a lower-level undergraduate student (freshman or sophomore) in the liberal arts, as this category was weighted at 1.00. It received $91.54 for every semester credit hour taught to a lower-level undergraduate in science, which had a weight of 1.64. And, it received $1,155.47 for every semester credit hour taught to a doctoral student in the sciences, which had a weight of 20.70. On top of that, Texas adds an additional weight of 10 percent to lower-division and upper-division semester credit hours taught by tenured and tenure-track faculty members. Of course, astute campus administrators cannot ignore the financial implications of these various weights when planning long-term enrollment and academic strategies.

Formula funding has its pros and cons. On the one hand, formula-based funding has two major advantages. First, formula funding introduces objectivity into the allocation process. Politics may be involved, but political influence will be expressed in the relative weights, not the application of the formula. Thus, by relying on quantitative algorithms for distributing revenue, the allocation process is not politicized at the department level. Second, formula-based budget models respond to changes in teaching loads, research productivity, or other formula parameters. Adjustments to formulas can promote internal funding equity and redistribute resources from shrinking to growing programs if they are applied symmetrically.

On the other hand, formula-based funding has two major disadvantages. First, unless performance measures are included in the formula, this model does not necessarily incorporate quality in the resource allocation process. Second, the formula-based allocations do not necessarily align with an institution's strategic plan. They may favor anomalous, non-strategic programs, which can raise discontent among slighted high-priority programs. Indeed, a differential weighting scheme, as in table 3.2, has the potential to pervert strategic planning. This can place the provost in the awkward position of having to override the strict formula-based allocations in order to conform to strategic goals.

Revenue-Based Budgeting

Revenue-based budget models allocate revenue generated by a budget unit back to the unit. Revenue is returned. Thus, they are called *revenue-based* or *activity-based* models. In a typical scenario, a college or department generates revenue for the university from five main sources (sometimes called "revenue lines"):

- tuition
- student fees
- grants and contracts
- indirect cost reimbursement
- outreach revenue (e.g., summer school, extension courses, workshops)

A revenue-based model returns to the college or department the revenue that it generates from each of these sources. In other words, revenues generated from instructional, research, and outreach activities are allocated directly to the unit responsible for the activity. This kind of model is described colloquially as "eat what you kill." (Endowment income is generally restricted, so it is not included in this scenario).

There is a significant catch, however: the provost usually imposes a tax on the returned revenue. Because of the tax, the budget units actually receive a fraction of the total revenue that they have generated. This tax is sometimes known as a *partici-pation tax* or a *participation fee*.[3] (The term "participation" refers to the budget unit's membership in the university, which enables it to use the university's name and goodwill). The provost uses the tax to supplement whatever other revenue might be available (such as state appropriations and endowment income) to pay for centrally provided institutional infrastructure, including the library, central administration, other indirect costs, and special programmatic priorities. The tax rate depends on the availability to the provost of income from other sources and the extent of the centralized infrastructural costs. Of course, from the units' perspective, the lower the tax rate, the better. Some institutions base the tax on a three- to five-year running average of past years' infrastructure expenses to smooth out unusual fluctuations in any single year.

In a revenue-based model, the provost or dean may supplement a unit's revenue return through subvention using funds derived from a variety of sources, including the participation tax, state appropriations, endowment income, licensing income, and interest income. Subvention is an important element of the model, because it provides a leverage point where the provost and deans can exert control over the allocation process; it keeps them in the game. For example, the campus subvention provides the opportunity to subsidize strategically important programs that cannot generate sufficient operating revenue through tuition or indirect cost reimbursement because they cannot accommodate large enrollments or compete for large federal research grants. Examples might include a school of architecture or an honors college. In addition, subvention provides the opportunity to reward or punish particular programs without selectively changing their percentage of revenue return, which is generally a bad idea. The same goal of rewarding or punishing a program can be reached simply by adjusting the subvention amount.

Depending on an institution's culture, the provost may or may not have sole discretion over the allocation of subvention funds. There are no general rules. However, it is safe to assume that most provosts do not make the decisions in a vacuum. They consult with various constituencies, such as other senior administrators and a campus budget committee, and adhere closely to institutional strategic plans when allocating subvention funds.

When preparing a budget like this, the first issue to settle is how to allocate tuition revenue. One way is to base tuition revenue generated by the college on the number of semester credit hours taught by the college relative to those taught by the entire university. If this share is 20 percent, then the college would receive 20 percent of the total tuition collected by the university. This approach implies that the college receives all of the tuition from courses taught by its faculty members. Another way is to base the tuition revenue generated by the college on the number of students majoring in departments within the college, recognizing that the departments attracted the students' interest and incur advising costs. So, if 20 percent of the students major in departments within the college, the college receives 20 percent of total tuition revenue. Of course, various hybrids of these and other possible approaches are possible.

As an illustration, a revenue-based return budget for a college is shown in table 3.3. For brevity, the prior year's budget (2019) has not been included in this example. Regardless of how the tuition revenue was calculated, the college is credited with $10 million in 2020. The provost imposes a 40 percent tuition tax (participation tax), leaving the college with $6 million, plus $400,000 in student fees that generally are not taxed. In the sponsored programs category, grants and contracts generate $7 million: $5 million and $2 million in direct costs and indirect cost reimbursement, respectively. The direct cost revenue is not taxed, because its use is restricted by the terms of the award. However, the unrestricted indirect cost reimbursement (primarily from federal

TABLE 3.3. *Revenue-based budget model for a college*

Revenue	2020
Tuition	10,000,000
Tuition tax (40%)	(4,000,000)
Student fees	400,000
Subtotal tuition and fees	6,400,000
Sponsored programs	
Grants and contracts	5,000,000
Indirect cost reimbursement	2,000,000
Indirect cost reimbursement tax (50%)	(1,000,000)
Subtotal sponsored programs	6,000,000
Outreach revenue	1,000,000
Outreach tax (40%)	(400,000)
Subtotal outreach	600,000
Subtotal net revenue	13,000,000
Campus subvention	1,250,000
Total net revenue	14,250,000
Expenditures	
Salaries and wages	9,000,000
Fringe benefits	3,000,000
Operating	250,000
Scholarships and fellowships	2,000,000
Total expenditures	14,250,000

grants and contracts) is taxed at a 50 percent rate. Likewise, outreach revenue generated by activities like summer school and extension is taxed at a 40 percent rate because these activities make use of university facilities and administrative services. Because of the taxes, earned net revenue ($13 million) is $1.25 million less than projected expenditures ($14.25 million). Consequently, the provost has added $1.25 million in subvention funds to balance the budget.

Looking at the numbers, the college paid $5.4 million in participation taxes and received $1.25 million in subvention. Therefore, the college's net outlay to the central administration was $4.15 million, which equals about 23 percent of its total (pre-tax) revenue, not including subvention. This percentage drops to about 22 percent when subvention is included in the revenue.

Notably, in this example, scholarships and fellowships are considered expenditures ($2 million), because the university issued the students cash, which they used to pay tuition. Alternatively, the university could have awarded the same amount of financial aid ($2 million) by discounting the students' tuition. This would reduce net tuition to $8 million and, therefore, the tuition tax to $3.2 million. On first thought, this alternative might seem to benefit the college financially. After all, it decreases the tax by $800,000. On further thought, however, it probably would not benefit the college financially because it would trigger a commensurately higher tuition tax rate to generate the revenue needed for the provost's subvention pool.

In general, revenue-based models provide strong incentives for the department to generate more revenue through teaching, research, and outreach activities. Presumably, the higher the percentage returned to the unit, the greater the incentive to generate more revenue. The University of Washington summarizes the broader advantages of a revenue-based model, stating that it empowers "greater local planning and accountability and creates incentives for units to manage resources and expenditures more efficiently. Further, direct control of resources generated from activities creates incentives to set priorities and develop new activities consistent with the overall mission and strategic goals of the institution."[4]

At the departmental level, revenue-based models also confer a more subtle advantage. By itemizing the sources of revenue, they document financial contributions to the department's budget from teaching and research activities. Sharing this information with faculty members tends to mitigate tensions between those whose primary activity is either teaching or research. For example, faculty members who no longer generate lucrative research grants often take on heavier teaching loads. The revenue-based budget information provides them the opportunity to point out how much more tuition revenue they generate for the department, perhaps leveling the financial playing field.

Responsibility Center Management

The decentralization inherent in the revenue-based budget model is expanded in *responsibility center management* (RCM). In this management-accounting model, each budget unit in the organizational hierarchy is considered a "responsibility center." By definition, "a responsibility center is a functional entity within a business that has its own goals and objectives, dedicated staff, policies and procedures, and financial reports. Such a center is used to tie specific responsibility for revenues generated, expenses incurred, and/or funds invested to individuals."[5] In an academic setting, this definition of RCM implies that each responsibility center—college, department, service center, and so forth—is responsible for its generated revenues and incurred expenses. Indeed, that is the core foundation of this budgeting model.

From a managerial point of view, the responsibility center director has the authority and the responsibility for managing all of the budget unit's revenues and expenses. This important point bears emphasis. The responsibility center director, such as a provost, dean, or chair, is responsible for managing all costs incurred by the center in the performance of its activities (teaching, research, and service). Appropriately, this responsibility is coupled with the director's authority to manage all revenue earned in the performance of these activities. Decentralization of responsibility and authority is a defining hallmark of RCM.

Within the university, there are two basic categories of responsibility centers: academic and administrative. The main attributes of the *academic responsibility centers* are the abilities to

- generate revenue
- cover direct costs with generated revenue
- cover fully allocated indirect costs
- retain both surpluses and losses

The academic responsibility centers encompass the colleges, schools, departments, centers and institutes, and other revenue-generating units. Some universities include auxiliary units, such as intercollegiate athletics, housing, and food services, in this category. In fact, auxiliary units are usually budgeted using the RCM methodology.

The *administrative responsibility centers* provide services that benefit the academic responsibility centers. These services are known as indirect services, and the costs of providing these services are considered indirect costs. Even the imputed cost of occupying a university-owned building—the equivalent of rent—is included as an indirect cost. In general, these units

- cannot generate revenue
- provide services and support to the academic responsibility centers
- are accountable for optimal service levels and fiscal performance

The administrative responsibility centers comprise financial services, registrar, buildings and grounds, information technology, human resources, and other support operations. Some institutions include resource centers such as museums, libraries, and theaters in this category.

In RCM, the academic responsibility centers must pay out of their revenue their share of the indirect costs incurred by the administrative centers. Unlike the other budget models, the central administration does not pay for the indirect services. Accordingly, like the revenue-based model, the RCM model allocates all revenues generated by the academic responsibility centers to the center. However, it also charges the academic responsibility centers for their use and consumption of indirect services, which appear in the budget as expenditures.

Ideally, all indirect services provided by the administrative responsibility centers could be charged directly to the user, and in some cases that is possible. For example, if each academic center's building has separate utility meters (for electricity, gas, water, internet access, etc.), then the indirect costs of these utilities can be billed directly to the center. However, this approach is not always possible or practical. In most cases, the indirect costs incurred by each responsibility center are based proportionately on some quantitative measure of their benefit to the center, such as assigned net square feet, salaries and wages, and student headcount. The institution calculates each responsibility center's share of the total indirect costs and expects the centers to pay for their share out of the revenues they have generated. For example, if the college of engineering uses 20 percent of the institution's total energy consumption, it pays for 20 percent of the total energy bill using revenue that it generated through its activities.

The RCM budget model shares two cardinal features of the revenue-based budget model: a participation tax and subvention. Like the revenue-based model, the RCM model imposes a participation tax on revenue to pay for common university costs, such as public relations, lawsuits, and common groundskeeping. Likewise, the RCM model depends on campus subvention to achieve a balance between responsibility center priorities and the best interest of the university as a whole. Funds in the subvention pool are used to supplement units needing assistance and to support university priorities.

Generally, the participation tax rates are less than in the revenue-based model. That is because the central administration does not require much, if any, tax to pay for the indirect services; those costs have been decentralized to the responsibility centers. Therefore, the RCM-based tax rate rarely exceeds 20 percent. Some universities, such as the University of Michigan, allocate state appropriations to fund the subvention pool, removing that liability from the participation tax. Relying on a single source for the subvention pool carries risk, of course. Because of subvention's importance in maintaining campus stability, best practice is to develop broad sources of revenue to fund the sub-vention pool continually, without major swings in the amount available.

Whether subvention is treated as a grant or a loan is a matter of campus policy. Most often, it is considered a grant and must not be repaid. Beware: as a grant, subvention carries the risk of becoming an entitlement, a sort of welfare. That should not happen. Subventions must be reviewed on a regular basis to ensure academic vitality. In this way, subvention resembles incremental budgeting.

Because they are self-sustaining budget units, responsibility centers generally control their fund balances. If revenues exceed expenditures, they retain the remaining positive fund balances, which can be carried over into subsequent years. In contrast, if expenditures exceed revenue, the negative fund balance must be repaid by reducing expenditures during the following year, dipping into positive fund balances from previous years, or borrowing from the provost with a promise to repay the loan from future years' budgets.

A prototypical RCM-based budget model, shown in table 3.4, illustrates how RCM expands on the revenue-based budget model (table 3.3). The actual revenues are the same for both models, but the participation taxes are considerably less in the RCM model. For example, the tuition tax decreases from 40 to 15 percent, which provides an additional $2.5 million in revenue in the RCM model. The decreased participation tax rates result in more net revenue in the RCM model: $16,500,000, compared with $13,000,000 for the revenue-based model. Likewise, the direct expenditures are the same for both models, $14,250,000. However, in the RCM model, the indirect costs of facilities (space, utilities, plant maintenance, and so forth), administrative support (central payroll, purchasing, and so forth), and the library are added to the college's expenditures, increasing total expenditures by $3.5 million. As a result, total expenditures ($17.75 million) exceed revenue ($16.5 million) by $1.25 million. To balance the budget, as in the revenue-based model, the provost has provided $1.25 million in subvention.

Again, looking at the numbers, the college paid $1.9 million in participation taxes and received $1.25 million in subvention. Therefore, the college's net outlay to the central administration was $650,000, which equals about 3.6 percent of its total (pre-tax) revenue, not including subvention. This percentage drops to about 3.4 percent when subvention is included in the revenue. These percentages are about 15 percent of those calculated for the revenue-based model (table 3.3).

In practice, of course, the RCM budget easily can become more complicated than this simple example, as other revenue sources are incorporated. They include endowments, gifts, state appropriations, licensing income, and auxiliary enterprises. Also, the tax basis for the subvention pool and the algorithms for calculating indirect expenditures generally vary between institutions, usually in attempts to account more accurately for differences in usage patterns among the different responsibility centers.[6] Typically, however, the facilities, administration, and library expenditures (that is, indirect costs) are allocated on the basis of standard metrics: square footage, total personnel (faculty and staff full-time equivalents), and total faculty members plus student enrollment in the fall semester, respectively.

All in all, RCM is an attractive budget model, for it creates a number of potentially powerful incentives. Because responsibility centers are responsible for meeting revenue projections and living within their planned operating margins, they have

TABLE 3.4. *Responsibility center management budget model for a college*

Revenue	2020
Tuition	10,000,000
Tuition tax (15%)	(1,500,000)
Student fees	400,000
Subtotal tuition and fees	8,900,000
Sponsored programs	
Grants and contracts	5,000,000
Indirect cost reimbursement	2,000,000
Indirect cost reimbursement tax (15%)	(300,000)
Subtotal sponsored programs	6,700,000
Outreach revenue	1,000,000
Outreach tax (10%)	(100,000)
Subtotal outreach	900,000
Subtotal revenue	16,500,000
Campus subvention	1,250,000
Net revenue	17,750,000
Expenditures	
Direct	
Salaries and wages	9,000,000
Fringe benefits	3,000,000
Operating	250,000
Scholarships and fellowships	2,000,000
Sub-total direct expenditures	14,250,000
Indirect	
Facilities	600,000
Administration	2,500,000
Library	400,000
Subtotal indirect expenditures	3,500,000
Total expenditures	17,750,000

incentives for growing new revenues, managing fund balances (both positive and negative) prudently, and limiting overhead costs by optimal space usage. Moreover, the decentralized nature of the model entrusts academic units with more control of financial resources, leading to more informed decision making and better results or outcomes for the university as a whole. By allowing responsibility centers to control the revenues they generate, colleges are better able to evaluate the academic and financial impacts of their decisions. For these reasons, numerous universities, including the University of Pennsylvania, Indiana University, and the University of Michigan, have adopted RCM, and the momentum suggests that more will do so in the near future.[7]

Despite its attractions, RCM has its detractors. They point out that the inherent competition between budget units for revenue undermines institutional integrity.[8] For example, they foresee departments offering duplicate courses to attract students such as "English for engineers" and "calculus for economics majors;" duplication of services to generate revenue; a decline in selectivity as colleges lower admissions and enrollment standards to boost tuition revenue; and departments discouraging students from changing majors because of lost revenue. Plus they foresee other potentially injurious side effects. Budget expert Leroy Dubeck (Temple University) summarizes his objections to RCM: "In short, RCM would pit the profit motive against academic considerations of which courses a student should take and where these courses could best be taught."[9]

These same concerns apply to any budget model that places incentives on student enrollments and course credit hours, including both the revenue- and the formula-based allocation models. They warrant attention, to be sure, although there are few anecdotal reports of abuse by predatory responsibility centers. Nonetheless, prudence dictates the need for central monitoring of these potential problems by the provost and the faculty senate.

Every Tub on Its Own Bottom

In the context of budget models, the extreme of decentralization is known as "every tub on its own bottom" (ETOB). Every school or college owns 100 percent of its revenue, runs its own central administration, and adheres to its own strategic plan. At most, they contract with the university for utilities, investment management, and perhaps financial accounting. Unlike RCM and other revenue-based models, ETOB does not rely on subvention to force investment in shared strategic objectives. For all intents and purposes, therefore, in ETOB the schools and colleges are independent members of an overall university-based federation.

Harvard University is the most prominent example. At Harvard, each school and college is fully dependent on its own revenues and in turn responsible for its own expenses. Operationally this results in a weak central administration. From a Darwinian perspective, individual units at Harvard must achieve financial self-sufficiency if they are to survive.

Few universities have adopted an ETOB model. This model is simply impractical for public universities that depend on state appropriations. Moreover, the extreme decentralization has proved to be an obstacle to efficient use of university resources in times of financial stress. Consequently, both the University of Pennsylvania and Vanderbilt University pulled back from the extreme decentralization of ETOB to the less extreme RCM.[10]

Static versus Flexible Budgets

In budgetary accounting, each of these budget models can be characterized further as either static or flexible. These terms describe the dynamics of the budget model. That is, they describe how the budgetary revenue allocations respond to market forces. Within the business community, market forces refer to demand for a product. Within the university, market forces refer to demand for certain courses, preferences for university dining halls, attendance at athletic events, and so forth. Usually, the levels of these activities are not known for certain when budgets are prepared, so they are based on projections.

A *static budget* remains constant, irrespective of the levels of activity. Accordingly, it is also called a *fixed budget*. Static budgets are based on educated guesses about future activity levels, such as enrollment per course, dining hall preferences, and football game attendance. Regardless of market-driven fluctuations in these activity levels during the fiscal year, revenue allocations and expenditure authorizations do not change. In business jargon, a static budget is created for a standard volume of production. For example, if enrollment in Accounting 101 increases by one hundred students in the fall semester, the business school must somehow accommodate the additional students without additional revenue added to the budget. Similarly, if football ticket sales drop by 20 percent, the athletic department must adapt its expenditures, for the lost revenue will not be added to the budget.

The main advantage of static budgets is that they set the revenue allocations for the year, simplifying planning processes. For example, in a static budget model, the costs of teaching Accounting 101 are set firmly at the beginning of the year. Beyond that point, the department must live within its means. Clearly, static budgets are best suited for budget units with few chances of significant fluctuations in their activities and with reasonable certainty about revenues and costs, barring extraordinary circumstances. Most university academic units (for example, departments), operate with static budgets that set revenues and expenditures for the fiscal year. Because it is not always possible to determine trends in student enrollment accurately, misjudgments must be corrected in future years' budgets.

In contrast, a *flexible budget* is designed to be adjusted easily. It is a financial plan created for different activity levels. If activity levels change, the budget can be revised to accommodate changing revenues and expenditures. Hypothetically, in a flexible budget model, the additional hundred students in Accounting 101 generate $50,000 in tuition revenue; correspondingly, authorized expenditures increase by $40,000, the amount needed to hire two additional instructors and teaching supplies. Conversely, if some other course, such as Finance 101 generates $50,000 less in tuition revenue than anticipated, the revenue allocation will decrease as fewer instructors are hired to teach the course. In either situation, the budget adjusts in response to the market forces. The adjustments may be entered automatically on the basis of a formula or manually on the basis of specific needs. In this example, a flexible budget is logical and practical because the revenue allocation follows the behavior of costs, distinguishing between fixed and variable amounts.

Clearly, the main advantage of flexible budgets is that they are responsive to changing market conditions. For that reason, they are best suited for budget units with highly variable activity levels affected easily by external factors or fluctuations in market conditions. Often, these budget units perform the university's core activities at the lowest level in the hierarchy, such as teaching undergraduate courses. (It is important to note that a low level in the hierarchy does not mean a low level of importance to the university.) Auxiliary enterprises that depend on customer demand, such as housing, dining halls, and intercollegiate athletics, particularly benefit from flexible budgets.

Pragmatically, operating budgets are neither purely static nor purely flexible. They are hybrids. For the most part, they are constructed a priori to be static. However, for activities affected by market fluctuations, such as teaching large undergraduate courses, the budgets must adapt flexibly. To control flexibility, some hybrid budgets incorporate several alternative revenue allocations based on specific activity levels such as the actual enrollment in specific courses or departments. The important point is this: ultimately, even in the most orthodox static budget model, reason must prevail.

Regardless of specific details, the budget model adopted by university policy guides the process for allocating revenue to the budget units. However, the models do not necessarily guide exactly how much is allocated to each budget unit. They leave open questions such as: Which requests for incremental funding or campus subvention should be approved? Except for the most explicit formula-based allocation paradigm, decisions must be made: Who gets how much? With the allocation in hand, the budget units must decide how to spend the money on their priorities. The next chapter describes the basis for those decisions.

Chapter 4

Strategic Plans

----

*S*trategic plans are an important prelude to the operating bud-get.[1] They document the university's aspirations for the future, what it wants to accomplish. Looking forward, they address questions such as: What is the university's vision? What are its ambitions for growth and programmatic development? The answers to these questions reflect the university's perception of the future.

To achieve these aspirations, strategic plans identify academic and operational priorities. Although strategic plans do not define these priorities in specific financial terms, they set the stage for the financial details inherent in the budget. The budget assigns resources to priorities identified in the strategic plan. Indeed, an effective budget must be predicated on an institution's well-defined priorities for accomplishing its mission, as defined in its strategic plan. In the planning jargon, the budget is *aligned* with the strategic plan.

The importance of the strategic plan to the budget is captured in a quip by the oft-quoted American baseball player Yogi Berra: "If you don't know where you are going, you might wind up someplace else." In the context of budget planning, it might be restated as, "If you don't know what your priorities are, you might spend your money on the wrong things." In that case, the items and monetary allocations in the budget may not line up with the university's priorities, thus diverting the university from its mission. As Yogi's quip implies, the university as a whole and its component budget units should have strategic plans that define their priorities and set their goals, and these plans must align with the budget.

The associations that accredit public and private schools, colleges, and universities support this assertion. They require universities to have strategic plans and to adhere to them. For example, in its *2013 Handbook of Accreditation*, the Western Association of Schools and Colleges (WASC) sets specific criteria for the "strategic thinking and planning" process, the alignment of priorities and resource allocation, and the assessment of these efforts: "The institution periodically engages its multiple constituencies, including the governing board, faculty, staff, and others, in institutional reflection and planning processes that are based on the examination of data and evidence. These processes assess the institution's strategic position, articulate priorities, examine the alignment of its purposes, core functions, and resources, and define the future direction of the institution."[2] The other accreditation associations have similar standards that they all take seriously. Indeed, failure to provide convincing evidence of a functional strategic plan can jeopardize accreditation reaffirmation.

The planning effort extends beyond the campus level into the lower hierarchical levels. Ideally, all budget units in the academic hierarchy develop a strategic plan that defines their priorities and goals within the context of the campus strategic plan. In that scenario, each college and department develops its own strategic plan that addresses its unique role in the university. These more focused strategic plans are part of the overall campus planning effort. Although they must adhere to the campus plan, they can be much more specific when dealing with internal priorities and operating procedures. For example, every year, the deans require department chairs to submit operational plans for the forthcoming academic year, addressing questions such as: What courses will be taught? Who will teach them?

Despite the management benefits of such plans, individual budget units lower in the hierarchy often do not have their own strategic plan. This failure may be due to lack of interest among the faculty members ("we're too busy teaching and doing research to bother with this kind of thing"), administrative inertia ("we just haven't gotten around to it"), perceived irrelevance ("we don't need a strategic plan to tell us what we need to do"), perceived helplessness ("what does it matter what we think?"), or a number of other imaginable reasons. Regardless, as a managerial best practice, individual budget units should be encouraged to develop their own strategic plan. As Steven Finkler and his coauthors assert in *Financial Management for Public, Health, and Not-for-Profit Organizations*, organizations that do not prepare an operational strategic plan "are often condemned to just sustain current activities at best."[3]

Because it is an important prelude to budget preparation, the planning process for a campus-wide strategic plan will be looked at through a budgetary lens.

Strategic Planning Process

The strategic planning process depends on the university's complexity. If the university is part of a multi-campus system, planning starts at the level of the system, which presumably has an overall strategic plan that defines the relationships between campuses and their separate missions. Individual campus planning derives from the system plan and involves mainly elaborating and refining the system plan. Campus plans must adhere to the tenets of the system plan, although the system's plan may be modified to suit an individual campus's unique character. If the university is not part of a multi-campus system, it can proceed with its strategic planning without the limitations imposed by a system.

The chief architects of the strategic plan include the administration and the faculty members. On the campus level, responsibility for preparing the plan and ensuring adequate consultation usually lies with the president's office, which may delegate it to the provost. On the college and department level, this responsibility falls on the deans and the chairs. The administration's influence over the plan's content depends on the institutional culture. At universities with strong faculty governance, faculty committees will do the planning and the writing. That is not an insult to the administration; it is a welcome benefit of an engaged faculty. In contrast, at universities with a limited number of engaged faculty members, the administration may be expected to prepare the plan's initial draft singlehandedly.

Regardless of who prepares a working draft, the draft plan must be vetted through extensive consultation with multiple constituencies. Comments are solicited from the broad university community, including alumni, external advisory boards, and members of the general public, who may tout the importance of some specific discipline or program. Of course, the number of constituents participating in the planning process scales down as the unit becomes smaller. But the general planning principles remain the same, and the preparation of these plans follows the same guidelines and process as the broader, campus-wide efforts.

Consultation is extremely important if the strategic plan is to be an effective tool for future decision making. It mitigates some of the inevitable controversy inherent in the priority-setting process. Stated in different terms, at every level in the academic hierarchy, the strategic plan must have *buy-in*. Furthermore, although some of the input may be irrelevant or impractical, as a best practice, the draft plan must be amended to accommodate meaningful input from the multiple constituencies. Otherwise, the plan's legitimacy can, and probably will, be called into question.

Buy-in competes with specificity. In the long run, however, as a cardinal premise, buy-in takes precedence over specificity; it is far more important than specificity. As a result, the consultative process may dilute programmatic specificity. That raises a penetrating question: What good is a watered-down plan that does not identify specific high-priority areas for future investment? In an ideal world, specific priority setting is the whole point of strategic planning, for it sets definitive guidelines for programmatic investment. From a practical perspective, though, experienced administrators can usually decide if a programmatic area adheres to a well-constructed plan that has little specificity, but they can never gain *post hoc* acceptance of these decisions without initial buy-in to the plan in general. Clearly, budget unit directors such as the provost cannot flout the strategic plan and interpret it however they want. That would be disingenuous. But if the final plan does not name specific priority areas, the operational goal in budgetary decision making is to try to honor the plan's spirit.

Despite broad consultation, some constituents may never agree with the strategic plan. Yes, they were consulted and provided input. However, their particular input may not have been incorporated into the final plan for one reason or another. This outcome can lead to cynicism and, at worst, a sense of helplessness that will seriously compromise the plan's usefulness as a budgetary guide.

> *Faculty member:* "I don't like your decision."
> *Provost:* "But it adheres to the strategic plan."
> *Faculty member:* "Whose strategic plan? Nobody listened to my input."

Unfortunately, in most situations like this, there are few simple remedies beyond compassion. Therefore, the importance of transparency cannot be overemphasized.

The planning process epitomizes the role of shared governance in university administration. Many people representing various constituencies have a say in the planning effort. That is good. Ultimately, however, the president and the provost will be held accountable for the campus strategic plan's success or failure. Likewise, the deans and chairs will be held accountable for the college and department plans' success or failure. Governance is no longer shared at this juncture. Therefore, the provost, for example, must be granted some flexibility in interpreting and implementing the plan. That does not mean that the provost has a license to ignore the plan when preparing the budget; on the contrary, the plan must be followed. The accrediting associations (and many observant faculty members and deans) keep an eye on that. Whenever major decisions deviate from the strategic plan, the provost, deans, and chairs must prepare justifications explaining why the decisions benefited the university. Watchful observers are more likely to allow reasonable flexibility in this regard if there has been meaningful consultation right from the beginning.

Sooner or later in the planning process, somebody must put the plan in writing: prepare the draft document, revise in response to feedback, and so forth. This responsibility often falls in the lap of an associate provost or a small group of faculty members serving as scribes for the larger planning community. The format varies according to institutional culture, but most strategic plans contain common skeletal elements. They will now be exemplified.

Strategic Plan Content

Campus-wide strategic plans start with *assumptions* about generic topics such as commitments to general education, diversity, state-of-the-art information technology, need-based financial aid, fiscal responsibility, and continual quality improvement. These basic topics underlie the plan and seldom evoke controversy.

They are axiomatic in nature and may not be incorporated specifically into the strategic plan document, but they are usually included as a preface or appendix.

Based on the assumptions, most strategic plans address four fundamental elements that characterize the university. These are its statements of

- vision
- mission
- values
- goals

The *vision* statement describes what the university aspires to do in the future. In a few words, it expresses the aspirations in broad, inspirational terms. For example, "the university will be recognized as a model educational institution that interweaves a liberal and practical education and as a top-tier research university." This brief statement sets the overall direction for the university for the next five years or so.

Unlike the vision statement, which projects into the future, the *mission* statement describes what the university does now. In that sense, it describes the reason for the university's existence, its raison d'être. In modern strategic plans, the mission statement is usually short (several sentences) and to the point. A hypothetical example captures the essence of a campus-wide mission statement: "The university's mission is to discover, preserve, and disseminate knowledge; produce creative work; and promote a culture of broad inquiry throughout and beyond the university community." A real example from the University of North Carolina is more specific: "The Graduate School of the University of North Carolina at Chapel Hill provides leadership to envision, shape and support the highest quality education for a diverse community of graduate students whose contributions will have global impact."[4]

Cynical critics might say that mission statements like these tritely state the obvious. Perhaps they do. Nonetheless, just to come up with these statements requires some thought about the mission. In that respect they prompt discussion about the university's, and in this example the graduate school's, fundamental reason for existence.

The *values* statement represents core beliefs and behaviors that define "who we are as an institution." As Cornell University puts it, the values "infuse all practices and activities within the institution."[5] Although core values vary between institutions, common tenets include

- excellence
- diversity
- respect for others
- collaboration
- integrity
- transparency
- trust

All members of the university community are expected to share these core values.

The *goals* statement describes the desired results of the university's efforts to achieve its vision, the object of its ambitions. Logically, these goals must conform to the core values. Usually, the strategic plan comprises four or five basic goals, each with several specific objectives to be met. Relationally, the goals describe *what* the desired results are, and the objectives describe *how* the university intends to achieve the goal: what and how. Three hypothetical goals illustrate this approach:

- Goal 1: Ensure a high-quality educational experience for students who will most benefit from it.
  - o Objective A: Provide a unique integrated freshman program involving the major colleges to build a common experience and identity for each incoming freshman class.

- o Objective B: Establish a solid curriculum for development of fundamental intellectual skills, including
writing, speaking, quantitative skills, analytical
reasoning, computing and information technology,
fine arts appreciation, and multicultural studies.
- Goal 2: Maintain and enhance world leadership in
research, scholarship, and creativity.
  - o Objective A: Expect all faculty members in academic
programs to maintain independent research projects
and to contribute to the dissemination of knowledge
through publishing, presentations, and other creative
endeavors.
  - o Objective B: Target areas of research excellence and
give special priority to programs where the university
has the opportunity to excel internationally because of
comparative advantages.
- Goal 3: Expand access through information technologies.
  - o Objective A: Require all programs to develop plans for
offering degree programs via asynchronous online
courses.
  - o Objective B: Expand online access to educational
resources used by faculty members and students in
teaching and research.

These goals and their associated objectives present explicit
courses of action to achieve the vision—a roadmap leading to the
future. Some universities add more detail to these goals. For example, they may include specific numerical targets and mile-
stones, with timelines for reaching them. In this way, they increase the resolution of the roadmap, but they do not change the
direction. Again, cynical critics might assert that these goals and
objectives offer little useful guidance. "What else would you
expect the university to do?" Perhaps they have a point. But,
stretching the metaphor further, a roadmap certainly reduces
the chances of getting lost along the way.

Predictably, controversy arises when the strategic plan's goals identify specific academic areas. Nearly every discipline or organizational unit will inevitably make its case for preferential consideration. Programs that are not identified will feel threatened or left out. Also predictably, such specificity complicates the planning process because of its implications for future resource allocations in the budget. To help navigate this bumpy road, it is useful a priori to emphasize the university's commitment to maintaining its existing highest-quality and most productive programs, even if they are not mentioned specifically in the strategic plan. Of course, this just makes good sense: do no harm. Disruptive tension between academic programs competing to achieve recognition as a high-priority area in the plan can be further mitigated by focusing the plan on areas where the institution has a comparative advantage owing to geography, location, history, ethnic or cultural features, and local economic conditions, to name a few. This makes good sense, too: play from strength.

Ultimately, specifying any single academic area may be politically unfeasible without broad compromises that greatly expand the list of priority areas. The areas may become very general, simply to minimize controversy. Instead of assigning priority to a specific field such as molecular biology, a plan may assign priority to a much broader field such as the life sciences or, even more generally, the sciences. Conceivably, some plan may emerge lacking any programmatic specificity. In practice, a broad, generalized expansion like this is quite acceptable to the provost, for it provides some wiggle room when aligning the budget and the strategic plan's priorities.

In their objectives, some universities may introduce numerical targets in a benign way that does not identify specific programs and therefore does not evoke controversy. For example, a university might assert that it is "committed to achieving a student body and faculty that reflects the racial and ethnic background of the community." Implicitly, to achieve this goal, some programs may be favored, but since no specific academic programs are named, there is little reason for controversy. Similarly, some universities set goals to increase enrollment or research activity by a certain amount: "The university will strive to increase enrollment to 20,000 students by 2025," or alternatively, "The university will strive to increase annual research expenditures to $450 million by 2025." Another numeric goal might be, "All of the university's research programs will be ranked in the top 25th percentile by 2028." It is relatively easy to come up with these sorts of nonthreatening numeric goals and to incorporate them into the plan. Consensus in this regard among the various constituencies comes fairly easily, because specific academic programs are not identified by name. The goals are lofty, and nobody has been left out.

More commonly, however, performance metrics and program specificity are components of a separate plan for implementing the strategic plan, sometimes called the implementation or the operational plan. The *implementation plan* may be an integral part of the strategic plan or a stand-alone document. Regardless, whereas the strategic plan establishes goals and broad strategies, the implementation plan establishes ways to achieve these goals. It drills down to detailed actions for making the strategic plan work, thus linking the strategic plan with day-to-day activities. It may identify specific numbers of new faculty to be hired, additional program support, reallocations of space, and so forth, often with timelines. However, the strategic and implementation plans seldom have specific financial numbers; rather, the dollar amounts are placed in the budget. In principle, therefore, the implementation plan forms the functional link between the strategic plan and the budget.

Alignment with the Budget

With the implementation plan in place, the budget can now be built on the framework of the strategic plan. The strategic and the financial plans come together in a process called *alignment,* which occurs during preparation of the budget as university resources are allocated to achieve the specific goals of the strategic plan. The budget follows the strategic plan's roadmap, and the university invests resources along the way. These investments, manifest as authorized expenditures in the budget, provide funding for the plan's various objectives en route to accomplishing the goals. This pertains to all university budgets: operating, capital, auxiliary, and project specific. The actual alignment process may vary between budget types, but the intended outcome is the same for each budget: expenditures target strategic goals.

Accordingly, to achieve goal 1, objective A in the hypothetical strategic plan described above, the university might use its operating budget to invest preferentially in departments offering core courses specifically for freshmen, such as the History of Western Civilization or Basics of Writing. In the capital budget, the university might invest in a dining facility where all resident freshmen take their meals. In its auxiliary budget the athletic department might even invest in free hotdogs and pizza for freshmen sitting in the freshman-only section of the football stadium. Similarly, other investments in the budget target the other objectives.

From a managerial perspective, alignment of the budget and the strategic plan is a crucial concept. Indeed, this alignment is fundamental to good management, not just in universities but in the business sector as well. It is what the accreditation associations expect of a university.

Before proceeding, it may help to recapitulate in logical order: the strategic plan defines the primary objectives the organization will undertake to achieve its mission, the implementation plan adds details to these objectives, and the budget allocates money to accomplish these objectives. Notably, in practice, smaller budget units may not have a formal implementation plan. Translation of the strategic plan to their budgets may be straightforward, with little apparent need for further detailed guidelines.

Strategic Plan Limitations

Ideally, a university develops a strategic plan and constructs a budget that implements the plan's strategic objectives straight-away. Unfortunately, reality quickly takes control of even the best-laid plans. Several examples will illustrate common limits to strategic planning efforts.

Changes in budget unit leadership may limit a strategic plan's effectiveness. For example, most strategic plans extend forward for five years or more. Over that period, changes in top leadership—the president, the composition of the govern-ing board, even the governor—can often trigger development of a new strategic plan before the old one has run its course. New leaders may argue for novel priorities that do not fall within one of the broad categories of the existing plan, or they may propose quite different ways to achieve the existing plan's goals. These changes can have a serious impact on the university's overall ac-ademic direction and can thoroughly disrupt ongoing imple-mentation efforts. They can also have a serious impact on bud-getary allocations. The provost, the deans, and even the chairs must be keenly alert to these possibilities whenever there is a major change in leadership and must be prepared to adapt quickly.

Many factors limit the attainment of numeric goals within a strategic plan. Although they are easy to incorporate into a stra-tegic plan, targets based on performance relative to other insti-tutions are particularly difficult to achieve because most other universities have a similar goal: to improve their standing in na-tional rankings. For example, consider the goal of becoming one of the top fifty universities in research expenditures by 2025. By that date, competing universities also will have increased their expenditures, so unless the institution's growth rate is faster than theirs, it will actually fall behind relative to them. The university may have successfully implemented its strategic plan. It may have increased its overall research activity—reflecting the true spirit of the strategic plan—but it did not move up in the national rankings. Unfortunately, success in achieving this kind of numeric goal depends not only on the university's efforts— no matter how valiant—but also on the success of competing universities' efforts. Unfortunately, the university has no control over that.

Likewise, achieving a targeted amount of research expenditures, such as $450 million by 2025, depends on uncontrollable factors. Federal funding priorities may shift away from an institution's strengths, the overall amount of extramural funding may drop (or not increase), one or more highly productive researchers may leave the university, to name a few. It takes little imagination to think up numerous other additions to this list. Most seasoned administrators recognize that it is not worth worrying too much about such factors beyond their control.

In comparison with these numeric goals, implementing a plan that invests in specific high-priority academic programs can be fairly straightforward—that is, in the best of conditions. However, two major shortcomings can limit the implementation of a strategic plan. The first involves money. Obviously, if money is in short supply, progress toward achieving strategic goals may be slow, and patience is required. Over time, however, incremental investments can generate meaningful results. The second involves size of the faculty and therefore the number of discretionary hiring opportunities. If a strategic plan calls for building up expertise in a particular area, the number of available faculty positions to be filled can become rate limiting. Large universities have an advantage over their smaller counterparts in this situation. For example, the biology department may have been awarded the funds to hire faculty in a campus-wide high-priority area such as environmental sciences. Unfortunately, the department desperately needs somebody to teach human anatomy to nursing students. The department's and the university's priorities do not match in this case. In a large university, the provost may be able to solve the dilemma by providing a second position to fill the anatomy teaching need, thus preserving the option to hire a high-priority environmental sciences researcher according to the strategic plan. This solution may not be available at smaller universities. Some institutions may also encounter serious difficulties in attracting qualified faculty members in popular fields.

There is an additional subtle aspect of faculty hiring involving money that limits strategic plan implementation. If the university recruits celebrated faculty (no matter what their rank) into its high-priority areas, their starting salaries may significantly exceed those of the existing faculty members. This all-too-common phenomenon is called *salary compression*. It raises an equity issue that budget unit directors usually cannot dismiss with just a shrug of the shoulders. The human resources office, the faculty union, or the governing board policies may insist on rebalancing an entire department's salary structure to relieve compression. How this is handled depends on the case and the university's culture. In these situations it is not unusual for the university to conduct a department-wide (if not even wider) salary study to ensure that the existing faculty members are treated equitably. This approach can result in additional salary costs. Incidentally, equity does not necessarily mean equality; equity studies take merit, time in service, and other factors into consideration.

Curiously, the subtlest impediment to implementing a strategic plan may be opportunism. Despite the strategic goal to hire new faculty members into some specific high-priority area in their department, the existing faculty members may prefer to hire a highly qualified individual in a different area who has become available. The rationale is this: "To build quality, we should always hire the best individual available." For example, although the posted job opening was for a high-priority biologist, a well-funded, highly regarded physicist just became available. *Carpe diem*; if opportunities arise, grab them. For many administrators, that is a difficult argument to counter. This is especially true for the dean or provost, who may be attracted by the thought of more research expenditures from somebody who is well funded, regardless of the strategic plan.

Thus, the debate ensues: Should a university simply hire the best person available in a broadly defined area, regardless of the strategic plan? Should hiring good faculty members in any area take precedence over the focused hiring into high-priority areas identified in the strategic plan? If the answer is yes, then why bother making a strategic plan? The answer lies in a metaphorical restatement of Yogi's comment: "You need to have some vision of where you're going, even if you don't always stay on the roadway." Again, big universities have all the advantages here. They have more hiring options, which mitigate the risks of occasionally straying from the strategic plan. Smaller universities with fewer hiring options risk compromising the strategic plan's effectiveness when they jump at opportunities regardless of the strategic plan.

Despite these limitations, a well-designed strategic plan constitutes the foundation for a university's budget. Conversely, the budget constitutes the vehicle for achieving the strategic plan's goals. Now, with a strategic plan in place, attention turns to the preparation of the operating budget per se.

Chapter 5

Operating Budget Preparation

----

lignment of budgets and the strategic plan occurs during preparation of the budgets. Because alignment of the budgets guides distribution of the university's money, an introductory question arises: Who aligns the budgets and the strategic plan? That question is tantamount to asking: Who prepares the budgets? The answer is important, because it tells who decides how much money each budget unit gets and what they can spend it on. Unfortunately, in the case of the operating budget, which typically commands the greatest interest among members of the academic community, the answer to this question is not straightforward; there is no single individual. Numerous individuals and groups usually participate in the preparation of both the strategic plan and the operating budget, obscuring the exact source of specific decisions about how the money is budgeted.

To shed light on this obscurity, this chapter examines each step in the process of preparing the master operating budget. A priori, however, it should be pointed out that universities also have processes for preparing capital and auxiliary budgets. The capital budget process is generally well defined (see chapter 2) but of marginal interest to most members of the academic community. The auxiliary budget process is less defined, mainly because auxiliary units are so varied and their budgets are more specialized. By and large, most auxiliary budgets are prepared by the auxiliary enterprise budget officer, in consultation with the unit director. The remainder of this chapter will concentrate on just the operating budget.

The Budget Process

When preparing the operating budget, universities typically follow a well-defined set of procedures known as the operating budget process or simply the *budget process*. Specifically, the operating budget process refers to construction of a university's master operating budget based on projected revenues and expenditures. Notably, the preparation of budgets lower in the hierarchy—in colleges and departments—is built into this budget process. This is when actual numbers are entered into the budget for specific items. So understanding the budget process is an important prerequisite to understanding how university budgets work.

Because of the inherent obscurity about exactly who prepares the operating budget, universities must strive to make the budget process as transparent as possible. An aphorism attributed to the Dalai Lama expresses it aptly: "A lack of transparency results in distrust and a deep sense of insecurity." Those words are as true in a university setting as in Asia. Therefore, as a best practice, universities should document the process, including tasks, responsibility assignments, and deadlines.

The Budget Cycle

With a strategic plan in place, the budget process proceeds in a two-phase cycle known as the *budget cycle*. Figure 5.1 illustrates the basic features of this cyclical paradigm.[1] In the first phase (right-hand side), revenues and expenditures are estimated and

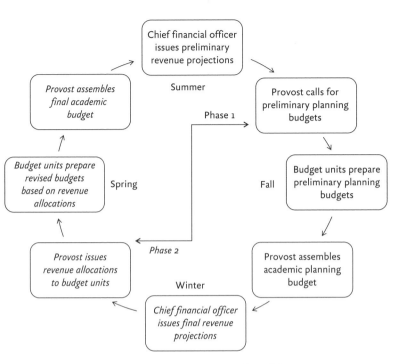

Figure 5.1. Academic operating budget cycle. Adapted from Dean O. Smith, *University Finances: Accounting and Budgeting Principles for Higher Education* (Baltimore, MD: Johns Hopkins University Press, 2019), p. 177.

items are proposed for inclusion in the budget. In the second phase (left-hand side), revenue and expenditure estimates are updated, the list of items in the budget is revised accordingly, and the consolidated budget is finalized. The entire cycle may take as long as about a year, as shown in figure 5.1, or as short as about six months, and it repeats itself annually.

Understandably, detailed aspects of the budget cycle will vary between universities. When defining their budget cycles, some universities may include additional steps or rearrange the sequence of steps. Nonetheless, this idealized version illustrates the basic skeleton of most budget cycles.

During the budget cycle, three major decisions must be made. The first decision is strictly financial: How much money will be available for the budget? The CFO has the primary responsibility for making this decision. The next decision evolves from the strategic plan: What items will be incorporated in the budget? The president and the provost have the primary responsibility for making this decision. Logically, the third decision evolves from the first two decisions, aligning the budget and the strategic plan: How much money will be invested in each budget item? The president, provost, and CFO work jointly to make this decision. Stated blithely, the president and the provost come up with the ideas and leave it to the CFO to come up with the money to pay for them. NACUBO describes the role of the CFO this way: "He or she must bring together the streams of revenue—unrestricted tuition dollars and other revenues, restricted funds available for spending, and endowment spending—with the plans of the institution, matching donor intent with actual spending in support of good stewardship and with fidelity to the gifts' requirements."[2]

The key elements of the cycle will now be examined more closely.

Preliminary Revenue Projections

Available revenues drive the budget cycle. After all, "you can't spend money you don't have." Therefore, the budget cycle begins with the CFO's issuance of preliminary revenue projections for the upcoming budget year (top of figure 5.1). These revenue projections must be accurate because they drive the entire budget cycle and therefore determine indirectly what items can be included in the budget and at what cost—that is, at what level of funding.

In an important preparatory step, the CFO analyzes the accuracy of current and past budget projections. Questions are asked. Did revenues and expenditures match expectations? Were some budget units clearly under- or overfunded? Are there any obvious corrections to be made in future budgets? With answers to these questions, the CFO establishes the informational context for the forthcoming projections. The primary concern is the accuracy, the certainty of the projections for the next year's budget.

The CFO arrives at revenue projections using two possible strategies: incremental and statistical. Depending on the size and financial stability of the institution, the CFO may use one or both ways.

Incremental Projections

As the term suggests, incremental projections are based on the previous year's revenue data. Basically, the past year's revenue is updated (incremented) to account for anticipated changes in the next year's revenue. In the simplest cases, the CFO gathers information about anticipated changes in revenue from each significant revenue source: tuition and fees, state appropriations, endowment income, investments, and grants (mainly indirect cost reimbursement).

Tuition and Fees

The enrollment management office updates the estimated gross revenue from tuition and fees, based on its enrollment projections for the next year. In an accounting context, the gross revenue from tuition and required fees equals the published tuition rates plus required fees times the number of full-time students (expressed as full-time equivalents, FTEs). The accuracy of these projections depends on the institution. Elite universities that have abundant applicants can project next year's enrollment with reasonable certainty. If acceptances are less than expected, they can admit more students from a waiting list. Universities that have marginal selectivity or open-enrollment policies (that is, they admit almost all applicants) must project enrollment more carefully, taking into account factors such as demographic trends, economic conditions, competing institutions, and other market factors. Their projections are necessarily less certain, so the CFO must consider them very conservatively. Indeed, for universities heavily dependent on tuition and fees as a revenue source, an unexpected enrollment drop as small as 1 or 2 percent can have significant financial repercussions.

The actual revenue from tuition and fees depends on the amount of scholarship allowances offered by the university, and that information is updated by the financial aid office. Quite simply, a scholarship allowance is the difference between the published tuition and required fees (the *sticker price*) and the amount actually charged to the student. In essence, it constitutes a grant of financial aid. As noted briefly in chapter 3, the scholarship allowance may be accounted for in two possible ways. On the one hand, if the institution provides students with institutional resources (for example, a check) that they use to pay part or all of their tuition, fees, or other expenses, the full tuition and fees (the gross revenue) are recorded as revenue, and the scholarship allowances are recorded as expenditures (illustrated in table 3.3). On the other hand, if the institution simply discounts the tuition and fees (that is, reduces the rates), the waived tuition and fees are subtracted directly from the gross revenue that might have been received in the absence of any discount. The scholarship allowance is *forgone revenue*, which is not reported as an expenditure. Stated colloquially, tuition discounting occurs when the institution charges a student less than its sticker price. Either way, the net tuition and fees received by the university are the full (gross) tuition and fees less the scholarship allowance. Because the institution can control the amount of scholarship allowance, the accuracy of projected net tuition and fees revenue usually differs little from the accuracy of the projected gross tuition and fees revenue.

State Appropriations

For public universities, state appropriations constitute an important source of revenue, yet universities have limited control over the magnitude of these appropriations from one year to the next. As the state legislature works its way through the appropriations process, university administrators testify regularly in budgetary hearings about the institution's financial needs. Often these hearings digress into discussions about programmatic priorities, out-of-state student quotas, and operational efficiencies, sometimes with political interests lurking in the background. As the legislative session progresses, the CFO gradually gets an idea about the next year's appropriation amount. In the best of situations, the final appropriation is known before the budget cycle begins, so the CFO has a firm number to work with. In some situations, though, the final appropriation may not be known with certainty before the next budget year begins. Consequently, the CFO must estimate the revenue from state appropriations for the preliminary budget. If the state's economy is stable, appropriation revenue estimates can be reasonably accurate, within about 1 or 2 percent. However, if the state's economy is unstable owing to declining economic conditions, the estimates can become uncertain. Indeed, in very bad economic conditions, appropriation revenue can decrease by as much as 20 percent or so after the university's budget year has begun. Needless to say, this causes serious financial stress.

Endowment Income

Endowment income originates from the return on the *long-term* investment of a university endowment's principal. Operationally, this income depends on the endowment's *payout rate*. The payout rate is the percentage of the endowment spent by a university in a given year. It equals the amount of the endowment spent by the university divided by the market value of the endowment. For example, if a university spends $4 million of endowment income and the market value of the endowment is $100 million, the payout rate is 4 percent.

The governing board (university or affiliated foundation, depending on management structure) sets the payout rate. The goal is to maximize the payout while reinvesting a sufficient amount of the return as a safeguard against inflation. As a buffer against market fluctuation, the payout rate is usually based on a three- to five-year average of the endowment's market value. It depends heavily on the balance between investment performance and institutional need. A positive investment performance and a constant budgeted need (for example, $10 million per year) translate to a decreased payout rate. Thus, counterintuitively, a university may report a lower payout rate during a time of lucrative investment returns. Conversely, a negative investment performance and a constant budgeted need translate to an increased payout rate. Depending on the circumstances, the university may increase the payout rate, thus reducing the reinvestment amount, or leave it constant, thus increasing the rate of principal growth.

The payout rate among universities is typically about 4 percent, although it may range from 3 to 6 percent. The Uniform Prudent Management of Institutional Funds Act (UPMIFA) considers a payout rate greater than 7 percent of the fair market value of an endowment fund a "rebuttable presumption of imprudence."[3] Therefore, payout rates seldom exceed 7 percent.

Because the university or its affiliated foundation sets the payout rate, the CFO can project with reasonable confidence the amount available for the next budget year. Again, in this context, the modifier "reasonable" means within about 1 or 2 percent. Quite probably, the university has determined the exact payout for the next budget year before the CFO prepares the preliminary revenue projections, thus removing uncertainty from projections of this revenue source.

Investments

Universities invest available cash in *short-term* investments. The amount invested varies considerably during the year. Some variation is predictable. For example, cash balances will spike at the beginning of each academic term as students pay their tuition and fees. However, some variation is unpredictable. For example, cash balances may drop considerably if damage due to a natural disaster (for example, a flood or earthquake) must be repaired quickly. In addition, some variation depends on the university's business acumen: How fast does it pay its bills and collect its accounts receivable?

This unpredictable variability limits the CFO's ability to project investment revenue with great precision. At best, the investment income generated during the past several years provides a basis for projecting the next year's investment income. Although the variability can be buffered by funds held in reserve, prudence dictates using the most conservative projection of investment revenue.

Grants

Grants generate revenue to pay for both direct and indirect costs. Although revenue for direct costs is factored into the budget, its use is restricted to specific grant-related activities. In contrast, revenue obtained from indirect-cost reimbursement is factored into the budget and, because it is unrestricted, is available to pay for all items in the operating budget. In research universities, this is an important source of revenue.

To estimate indirect-cost reimbursement in the next fiscal year, the CFO customarily requests grant-revenue projections (and any unusual expenditure projections) from each budget unit: the deans, directors, chief research officer, and so on. This requires principal investigators to predict how many of their grant proposals will be awarded. On the one hand, for awards already funded, predictions are easy to make. Deviations from

the amount awarded for indirect costs can occur only when direct costs are re-budgeted. For example, if a salary that incurs
indirect costs is re-budgeted to a piece of equipment that does
not incur indirect costs, then the indirect-cost reimbursement
will decrease accordingly. On the other hand, for proposals not
yet funded, the predictions are plagued with uncertainty.
Indeed, with many federal agencies awarding only about 20 to
25 percent of all proposals, the prospects of success are indeter-
minate. Furthermore, if a grant is awarded, further questions
arise: Will the requested budget be funded in full or reduced
by the granting agency? And if it is reduced, what items will
be trimmed and how will they affect indirect-cost reimbursement? For most principal investigators, these questions about
pending proposals simply cannot be answered with certainty,
so their predictions are equally uncertain. Nonetheless, after
consulting with their principal investigators, the department
chairs submit their best estimates of reimbursable indirect costs
to the CFO.

Ultimately, the CFO consolidates the projections from all
revenue sources, comparing them with previous years' actual
numbers. Senior, experienced financial officers usually have a
fairly good sense of the accuracy of these projections and may
tweak the numbers up or down. Prudently, they always favor
the lowest estimates of the next year's revenue.

Statistical Projections

In alternative methods, statistics are used to forecast revenues
and expenditures.[4] In the simplest method, standard least-
squares regression calculations are used to fit a straight line to
total revenue or expenditure amounts from the past several
years, and the line is extrapolated to the upcoming budget year.
The extrapolation yields the projected values. Theoretically, if
the budgets were perfectly in balance each year, revenues and
expenditures would be equal each year. In that case, the projected values would also be equal. Usually, however, revenues

and expenditures are not equal by the end of each year, so their projected values are not expected to be equal.

The outcome of these statistical projections depends on the number of past years used when fitting the regression line. Shorter time periods (such as two or three years) reflect recent trends, and longer time periods (such as four or more years) reflect historical trends. Therein lies the art of statistical projections: choosing the appropriate number of years in the past for the regression. The CFO must make that decision based on the stability of financial conditions over the past several years. If revenues have fluctuated more in the past year or two than in preceding years, then the CFO would likely fit the straight line to only the past two or three years. Regardless of the number of years analyzed, a prudent CFO would probably issue the lowest revenue projection as the target in the preliminary budget.

The advantages of the linear regression method are that it reflects statistical trends, short term or longer term. It looks beyond one-time anomalies in revenue or expenditures. That is also, however, its main disadvantage; the regression does not account for one-time circumstances that might affect the next year's revenue or expenditure projections. It is blind, so to speak, to a stock market crash or natural disaster that affects university revenues. In that sense, linear regressions are more suitable for long-term projections. Accordingly, they (and more sophisticated statistical techniques) are used primarily for long-term forecasting by large organizations and government agencies (such as the U.S. Office of Management and Budget). Although the statistical method removes human bias from the projections, in practice it should be used in conjunction with—not in lieu of— the more conventional incremental projection method.

Flexible Projections

Regardless of the method used, revenue projections harbor uncertainty. To mitigate significant uncertainty, the CFO may introduce flexibility into an otherwise static budget. A common strategy is to adopt several alternative revenue projections: *flexible projections*. For example, facing unstable enrollment projections, the CFO may issue three alternative revenue projections, with revenues set at $50 million, $52 million, and $54 million, which will result in the need to prepare three budgets. As enrollment stabilizes, the revenue projection may settle in on one of the three alternatives. Willamette University exemplifies this approach: "To minimize risk in an uncertain and volatile economic environment, we created a three-tiered, contingency budget with three funding levels based on enrollment performance. Most important, the budget—despite its tripartite contingency funding—fully reflected a set of core goals approved by the trustee and faculty budget committees and supported by the faculty."[5]

Expenditure Projections

In general, revenues determine expenditures. If next year's revenue is projected to increase, then next year's expenditures are projected to increase by about the same amount. In other words, expenditure projections track revenue projections. As a result, while preparing revenue projections, the CFO is also preparing expenditure projections. In that sense, there is little need to project the amount of planned expenditures; they cannot exceed the available revenue.

Nonetheless, for planning purposes, expenditures for specific line items must be projected for the next budget year. The main reason is to ensure that planned expenditures do not exceed projected revenues. As with revenue projections, the primary concern is accuracy. Fortunately, some planned expenditures are stable and probably will not change much during the fiscal year. For example, expenditures for tenured faculty members are reasonably stable during the year. Unfortunately, others are less stable and can change unpredictably during the fiscal year, but they are usually not as costly as salaries. For example, utilities and snow plowing are less predictable. The amount of money is small compared with salaries, but the CFO must nonetheless take the variability into account.

Statistically, personnel costs introduce the greatest variability into the CFO's expenditure projections. The reason is straightforward. Overall, 72 percent of all expenditures are for employee compensation: salaries, wages, and fringe benefits.[6] Moreover, 92 percent of total instructional expenses are for employee compensation. Accordingly, when forecasting expenditures, the CFO analyzes anticipated changes in institutional hiring plans, retirements, unpaid leaves of absence, and so forth. The data for these analyses come primarily from the provost and the office of human resources. The remaining noteworthy expenditures are for supplies and services, with a relatively small (but programmatically important) amount for scholarships and fellowships. Notably, the high percentage of expenditures required for salaries in the instructional budget leaves little slack for adjustments in these other categories to accommodate declining revenue projections due to reduced state appropriations, decreased endowment income, or sharply declining enrollment.

Looking forward, the budget must adjust expenditures for inflation. Otherwise, budgeted expenditures for some items may not be sufficient to accommodate higher costs due to inflation. There are two measures of inflation: the Higher Education Price Index (HEPI), calculated by the Commonfund Institute, and the Consumer Price Index (CPI), calculated by the U.S. Labor Department.[7] In 2016, their calculations showed that inflation increased by 1.8 percent and 0.7 percent relative to 2015, respectively. Because it focuses on university expenditures, the HEPI estimate is more reliable in this context. Moreover, the Commonfund Institute itemizes expenditures by eight institution types, nine regions in the country, and eight expenditure categories: faculty, administrator, clerical, and service employee salaries; fringe benefits; supplies and materials; and utilities. With this level of detail, the CFO can project inflationary adjustments with reasonable accuracy. And, of course, hoped-for pay raises must be taken into account.

In some extraordinary cases, projected expenditures drive revenue projections. These are "man-bites-dog" situations that occur when extraordinarily costly expenditures loom on the horizon, requiring significantly more revenue than in previous years. For example, the one-time costs of repairing damage due to a natural disaster such as an earthquake, hurricane, flood, or fire may require a significant increase in the next year's revenue. The extra revenue needed to pay for these expenditures must be found somewhere. Some long-term repairs may be incorporated into the capital budget, spreading the cost over many years. However, for more immediate repairs included in the operating budget, the next year's projected revenue may require inclusion of one-time supplements from sources such as reserve funds.

Preliminary Planning Budgets

With the CFO's preliminary revenue and expenditure projections in hand, the provost moves to the next step, issuing calls to each budget unit for preliminary planning budgets. The provost asks each unit to prepare a budget, based on these preliminary projections, that aligns with the unit's strategic plan. If the CFO issued flexible revenue projections, the provost may ask the budget units to prepare budgets for each revenue scenario. Or, conservatively, the provost may ask the budget units to prepare budgets adopting only the lowest revenue projections. Regardless of how many budgets must be constructed, they must all reflect the university's and the budget units' strategic priorities. That is, they must all align with the strategic plans.

Philosophically, there are two approaches to this preliminary budget planning process. On the one hand, the provost may issue rather strict guidelines about the process, thus limiting a budget unit's options. This approach tends to standardize responses from the various budgetary units, enhancing efficiency.

But it tends to maintain the programmatic status quo, limiting academic innovation. On the other hand, the guidelines may be less restrictive, leaving open the opportunity for the budget units to include proposed expenditures that exceed the revenue that they can reasonably expect to get. Although this pie-in-the-sky approach might seem unrealistic, it promotes thoughtful planning for future program growth and quality enhancement. On a cautionary note, when adopting this permissive approach, the provost must also take steps to manage expectations to avert morale-busting disappointment when some proposed expenditures ultimately are not included in the final budget.

These preliminary budgets then flow up to the top of the academic hierarchy. Starting from the lowest-level budget unit in the hierarchy, preliminary budgets are submitted to the next-higher level, where they are reviewed for consistency with guidelines and strategic objectives. The budgets from each unit at that level are then consolidated and submitted to the next-higher level and so forth, up the organizational hierarchy to the level of the provost. For example, the deans consolidate the departmental budgets and their own priorities into an overall school or college budget that they transmit to the provost, who consolidates them along with the budgets from other units reporting to the provost into a campus academic planning budget.

Similarly, other vice presidents also prepare preliminary operating budgets for their branches of the university. Commonly, they include the vice presidents for finance and administration, student affairs, and research. The athletics department may also be a separate budget unit in this category.

Finally, the provost and the other vice presidents submit their consolidated operating budgets to the university's chief budget officer, who once again reviews them for consistency with guidelines and strategic objectives. After any inconsistencies have been corrected, the budget officer consolidates the budgets into an institutional consolidated planning budget that goes to the president and possibly the governing board for information and approval. At this stage, the approval merely authorizes the budget office to continue to the next phase of the budget cycle (phase two), which involves preparation of the final consolidated budget.

Final Revenue Projections

By the time the president and perhaps the governing board review the preliminary planning budget, several months will have passed since the CFO issued preliminary revenue and expenditure projections. During that time, revenue and expenditure projections for the next year will have become more precise. Potential students accept or decline offers of admission, state legislators close in on final appropriation amounts, departments conclude faculty hiring for the following year, grant proposals are awarded or rejected, and so forth.

Although there is still an element of uncertainty, at some point in time the CFO issues final revenue and expenditure projections for the next year. This marks the transition from phase one to phase two of the budget cycle, the transition from a preliminary planning budget to the final operating budget.

Revenue Allocations

Based on the CFO's final revenue projections, the provost must decide how to allocate revenue. As with the preliminary revenue projections in times of financial uncertainty, if the CFO issues several alternative final revenue projections, the provost presumably passes along the alternative revenue allocations to the deans and, therefore, the department chairs, requiring them to prepare different final budgets for each revenue scenario. Realistically, the departments probably will have to settle for the lowest revenue projection, with the hope that they will benefit if funding levels increase. However, whether the provost actually passes along any future funding-level increases to the deans depends on institutional policy and culture.

In general, revenue allocations are constrained by the campus budget model. Therefore, if the campus adheres to a formula-based model, the provost has little discretion in how revenue is allocated. In contrast, if the campus adheres to a zero-based or incremental budget model, the provost has considerable discretion in allocating revenue. If the campus adheres to a revenue-based model, which lies between these two poles, the provost has some discretion, but it is limited to the amounts of the participation fee (that is, the tax on revenue) and any campus subvention.

With the possible exception of strict formula-based revenue allocations, provosts usually have the authority to make decisions about revenue allocations singlehandedly. However, they commonly seek the advice and support of a consultative budget committee composed of faculty members, staff, and perhaps students. This committee plays an important role for two reasons. First, it generates buy-in by involving members of the university community in construction of the final budget. Second, it incorporates the "wisdom of the crowd" into the decision-making process. Allegedly, such an approach results in decisions that are better than those that could have been made by the provost alone.[8] It must be remembered, of course, that the budget committee is consultative. For that matter, the provost serves at the pleasure of the president, and the president serves at the pleasure of the governing board. Ultimately, therefore, the governing board retains final decision-making authority and responsibility.

Before making final allocations, provosts commonly hold *budget hearings* for each academic budget unit. The budget hearings play a significant role in the decision-making process. In these hearings, the budget unit directors have the opportunity to defend their budgets by presenting their unit's strategic goals and needs to the provost and the budget committee. Predictably, the deans, for example, lobby for increased support, stressing the importance of their unit's contributions to the university and its strategic plan. Presumably, the provost and the committee members weigh the information obtained in these hearings as they finalize the budget, aligning resources with strategic-plan priorities. They may withhold resources for some items, but seldom will they add resources for items not in the preliminary planning budget. (That would constitute inappropriate micromanagement.)

The budget hearings consume a lot of time and effort for the budget unit directors, the committee members, and the provost. Are these hearings worth it? The answer is a qualified yes. Realistically, from a financial perspective, the hearings usually do not make a big difference for most budget units. They tend to emphasize four main themes common to many strategic plans: maintaining core academic programs and activities, sustaining competitive salaries for faculty and staff, managing financial aid in order to maintain a diverse and academically talented student population, and ensuring that academic facilities support the educational mission. Also, the provost probably has preconceived notions about which units warrant additional investment. Moreover, the amount of discretionary revenue available to the provost is usually quite limited. Consequently, for most units, the hearings do not affect the amount of incremental change in their budgets. Only the few units with the most convincing presentations in the hearings may receive a meaningful financial benefit from the hearings.

Nonetheless, despite these realistic limitations, from a programmatic perspective the budget hearings play an important role for all budget units. They provide an impetus for the deans and department chairs to think deeply about their unit's academic plans for the next year, to figure out where they are going. And the hearings provide the opportunity to communicate and vet these plans with the committee and provost. Overall, this exercise is important for the university's academic vitality.

Ultimately, the provost decides on final revenue allocations for the schools and colleges and issues them to the deans, who have likely been going through similar decision-making processes in their individual budget units. Indeed, like the provost, the deans also may have consultative budget committees and budget hearings for each department. Accordingly, the deans pass final revenue allocations down the hierarchy to the departments, which in a similar pattern have been making decisions about their own revenue allocations within the department. At each level, the units revise their preliminary planning budget based on their final allocated revenue and programmatic priorities. These revised budgets, which match planned expenditures with available revenue, then flow back to the top. The deans assemble their department budgets into an overall school or college budget that they transmit to the provost.

Final Budget Assembly

At this last stage of the budget cycle, the provost consolidates the deans' budgets into the final academic budget. In the process, the provost reviews each submission for accuracy, consistency, adherence to guidelines, and alignment with the campus strategic plan. Usually, this review is not perfunctory. The provost may request emendations of one sort or another. When the provost is satisfied with the final budget, it is passed on to the CFO, who in turn consolidates it with the budgets from other vice presidents, thus assembling the institution's consolidated, master operating budget.

If the university is part of a multi-campus system, there is the additional step of consolidating the budgets of each campus, this time by the system CFO. Likewise, for public universities, there may be yet another step of consolidating the budgets of all public universities into the state budget. After all of these consolidations rise up the hierarchy, the final institutional budget is called the consolidated budget for good reason.

At the conclusion of the consolidation process, the CFO (via the president) submits the consolidated operating budget to the governing board for approval. Although the board may spend considerable time discussing the consolidated budget, it seldom withholds approval. It should be pointed out, however, that the CFO, president, and the provost usually communicate routinely with key members of the board during the budget cycle, keeping them up to date on the budget process and resolving any contentious issues well before the final vote of approval. (Boards try to avoid any display of disagreement or disunity with the administration or among themselves in public meetings.) What might be contentious? The list is long when the budget is declining: Why do we continue teaching Latin and Greek? Does this small state really need a medical school? Should we discontinue Division I varsity football? Anecdotally, governing boards tend to focus their attention on relatively small-ticket items in the budget, low-hanging fruit of particular local interest to one or two board members. Indeed, the president of a Big Ten university once quipped that the board spent more time quibbling about a $25,000 research project than the financially beleaguered university hospital, which was running multimillion-dollar budget deficits annually. Anecdotes aside, aware of their fiduciary responsibility, governing boards review budgets assiduously.

Despite its tedious nature, the budget process is important to the viability of an organization. This importance is recognized by the regional accrediting associations, which have a common standard requiring the alignment of resources—that is, the budget—with educational purposes and objectives. For example, the Southern Association of Colleges and Schools Commission on Colleges requires an institution to have "an annual budget that is preceded by sound planning, is subject to sound fiscal procedures, and is approved by the governing board."[9]

Because of the important role the budget process plays in the university, numerous books and articles have been written about it.[10] Each provides a unique approach to the topic, but at their core they all emphasize the basic features summarized by Elizabeth Hamilton Foley in a tutorial on nonprofit accounting basics:[11]

> The budget process is the way an organization goes about building its budget. A good budgeting process engages those who are responsible for adhering to the budget and implementing the organization's objectives in creating the budget. Both finance committee and senior staff participation is built into the process and a timeline is established leaving adequate time for research, review, feedback, revisions, etc. before the budget is ready for presentation to the full board. The annual budgeting process should be documented, with tasks, responsibility assignments and deadlines clearly stated. A good budgeting process also incorporates strategic planning initiatives and stipulates that income is budgeted before expenses. Fixed costs are identified and related to reliable revenue. Budgeting decisions are driven both by mission priorities and fiscal accountability.

With the final budget in place, attention now turns to implementing the budget, making it work. This is not always a simple task, as will be shown in the next chapter.

Chapter 6

Budget Implementation

It would be natural to imagine that the budget document provides sufficient guidance for spending the university's money. For example, if a department budget has a line item that allocates $1 million for faculty salaries, then the department should be able to spend $1 million for faculty salaries with no questions asked. After all, the expenditure authorization was vetted and approved by the dean, provost, president, and governing board.

But reality is seldom so simple. Indeed, numerous complications of one sort or another inevitably disrupt simplicity. They range from unexpected revenue shortfalls to unanticipated major expenditures. Furthermore, myriad minor complications inevitably arise during the year. Metaphorically speaking, the budget establishes map coordinates. The pathway between coordinates may simply be straight or, far more commonly, complicated by roadblocks, detours, and shortcuts. To make the budget work, these complications must be accommodated. The need for these accommodations introduces the topic of budget implementation.

Implementation

Budget *implementation* refers to the process of putting the budget into effect, of executing the plan inherent in the budget. The final, consolidated operating budget brings together the results of planning activities throughout the campus, aligning programmatic priorities and the available revenue. In this context, the budget represents a plan. To accomplish the plan's goals, the available revenues must be spent according to the budget's guidelines—the budget must be implemented.

Budget implementation requires constant administrative attention. The task falls broadly into the budget office, which is in the CFO's realm. In fact, however, budget implementation usually dominates the daily workload of all budget unit directors lower in the hierarchy: the provost, deans, department chairs, and so forth.

Procedurally, budget implementation involves three key steps:

- release of funds
- control of revenues and expenditures
- budget modifications

Each of these implementation steps contains ways of correcting deviations from the budget, from the plan, that result from unpredicted variations in revenue or expenditures.

Release of Funds

With a final budget approved by the governing board, the stage is set for the CFO to release funds for expenditure in the new fiscal year—or, more technically, the stage is set for the CFO to delegate authority to commit university funds. This delegated authority percolates down into the hierarchy to each budget unit. For intuitive clarity in the budget context, the phrase "release funds" will be used interchangeably with "delegate authority."

When releasing funds authorized in the final budget, the CFO exerts financial control over two key aspects that provide opportunities to accommodate unpredicted fluctuations in revenue or expenditures: the timing of the release and the actual amounts released.

Apportionment

The CFO controls the timing of the release of funds to the budget units through a practice known as *apportionment*. As a matter of prudence, CFOs usually release funds in periodic allotments, or apportionments, rather than all at once. For example, they may release one-fourth of the budgeted funds each quarter. Similarly, in step-like fashion, the provost and the deans release funds to their constituent units in periodic apportionments. This is good practice. Under stable financial conditions, the periodic timing of the releases does not pose significant challenges. Personnel salary and student financial aid commitments for the entire year can be made with reasonable confidence that the necessary funding will be forthcoming. Under unstable financial conditions, the periodic timing of the releases makes it easier for the institution to adapt financially to unanticipated changes in revenue or expenditures. For example, apportionments can be reduced if the available revenue falls short of projected amounts during the fiscal year owing to a drop in enrollment in the second semester or a state tax shortfall.

On the downside, the periodic apportionment process constrains flexible use of the money. For example, the total amount of money needed by a department for an opportunistic expenditure in the first or second quarter may not be available until the third or fourth quarterly apportionment. In those cases, the department chair would presumably ask the dean for an advance allocation to take advantage of the opportunity.

Underallocation

The CFO also limits the actual amount of funding released, often through a practice known as *underallocation*. Most CFOs seldom release the entire amount authorized to the budget units. Instead, the CFOs retain a fraction in a *contingency fund* to address unforeseen circumstances. In other words, they underallocate revenue. Like the CFO, the deans and department chairs also commonly underallocate their apportionment, retaining a fraction of the funds released to their budget units in a contingency fund to buffer any unexpected decreases in subsequent fund releases during the year and to provide a source of discretionary money for items not in the budget. The contingency funds resulting from underallocation improve the university's financial stability by providing sources of money to meet emergency needs.

Significantly, underallocated funds and unspent contingency funds may also be transferred to a *reserve* account. Contingency funds differ from reserve funds. Contingency funds are set aside for short-term unexpected purposes, and reserve funds are set aside for specific long-term planned purposes such as repaying debt or repairing and replacing capital assets. There is a caveat: in financial crises, reserve funds may be used to cover significant unplanned revenue shortfalls or expenditures.

The amount underallocated for a contingency fund is usually 3 percent or less of the operating budget. So if a college budget authorizes $10 million in expenditures, the dean may allocate only $9.7 million to the department chairs, keeping $300,000 (3 percent of $10 million) in a contingency fund. Some institutions limit underallocation to the non-salary portions of the operating budget. In those cases, if salaries and non-salary expenditures comprise 70 and 30 percent of the college's $10 million budget, amounting to $7 million and $3 million respectively, the dean would underallocate $90,000 (3 percent of $3 million) for a contingency fund.

Like reserves, contingency funds attract attention, sometimes critical. From the point of view of a CFO, provost, dean, or department chair, contingency funds make sense. They buffer the revenue stream by providing a modicum of discretionary funding. But from the point of view of a faculty member, contingency funds tie up money that could otherwise support the academic mission directly: money for faculty salaries, curricular support, student financial aid, travel. This criticism is amplified by any perception that contingency funds are not used when they are needed, that they are being hoarded. Consequently, as a best practice, budget units should spend contingency funds liberally but wisely during the fiscal year, resisting any tendency to maintain a growing balance that carries over from year to year.

Recapture

As an alternative to underallocation, some universities establish contingency funds through a practice called *recapture*, or reversion. Recapture means that all of the funds authorized in the budget are released, but then during the fiscal year budget units are required to return unexpended money to the next-higher level in the hierarchy. For example, a dean returns a fraction of the authorized college budget to the provost. Consequently, the dean ends up with less spending authority than in the original budget, and the provost ends up with contingency funds. In other words, the provost recaptures a fraction of the college's authorized budget. Accordingly, *recapture funds* refer to unspent funds that have already been approved in the budget for a particular use but have been taken back to pay for a different use— they have been repurposed.

Recaptured funds commonly result from personnel vacancy savings, sometimes called *lapsed salaries*. The savings derive from budgeted amounts for faculty, administrative, and staff positions that are not expended because a faculty or staff member has vacated a position. This includes savings from salaries, fringe benefits, pay raises, and any other costs not spent because of the vacancy. The lapsed-salary savings may accrue because the position is left unfilled for part or all of a fiscal year or because the position is filled on a temporary basis at a salary rate less than the budgeted amount.

If a position becomes vacant, the position number may be recaptured as well. In the strictest institutions, vacant position numbers and the resulting savings revert automatically to the next-higher level in the hierarchy. Procedurally, if a faculty member leaves the university, the position and its associated salary revert from the department to the dean and sometimes directly from the department to the provost, sidestepping the dean. The department must then apply for the authority to hire a replacement. The likelihood of receiving that authority depends on competing demands for the money. The department's needs may justify the authority to hire an immediate replacement to meet teaching, research, or service obligations. However, the dean may return a position number but only at a lower job-classification level on the premise that a replacement can be hired at a lower salary. For example, if a full professor earning $100,000 a year vacates a position, the dean may recapture the position number and the entire salary but then return an assistant professor position number and only $60,000 in salary. Or the dean may not return the position or salary at all. In that case, they are lost to the department's budget. (But they are not lost to the department's memory. For many years, departmental old-timers will complain that the department is "down one position.")

In the most lenient institutions, the position number and the salary savings remain in the department. There is no recapture. The department may recruit a replacement immediately or leave the position vacant for several years, using the lapsed-salary savings for other purposes such as graduate student support. Less lenient institutions may recapture the salary but not the position number. In those cases, if a faculty member vacates a position, the dean recaptures only the salary until the department hires a replacement. At that time, the replacement's salary is returned to the department's budget.

The strict and lenient procedures have both pros and cons. In strict institutions, on the pro side, recapturing the lapsed salary savings provides the provost or deans opportunities to reallocate funding to higher-priority programs at the college or institutional level. This enables the university to respond quickly to changing demands. For example, if enrollment in the accounting department's entry-level Accounting 101 course exceeds projections, the dean can use salary savings from other departments to hire additional instructors to meet the demand. However, on the con side, knowing that they may lose a vacant position number, a department may lower its performance standards for renewing employment contracts and awarding tenure. In lenient institutions, on the pro side, keeping the salary savings provides departments the opportunity to reallocate funding to higher-priority activities within the department. For example, the department may leave a faculty position vacant, using the salary savings to raise graduate student stipends or equip laboratories. Also, it allows the department to make rigorous promotion and hiring decisions without fear of losing the position number if it is vacant. However, on the con side, this leniency favors financial status quo. Worse than that, leaving a faculty position vacant for more than a year or two brings into question the department's need for the position. Theoretically, the lenient strategy is more conducive to academic quality, but it comes at the cost of academic flexibility.

Control of Revenues and Expenditures

Proper implementation of the budget requires vigilant control over revenues and expenditures to avert unwarranted deviations from those that have been authorized. Stated more bluntly, the university must have controls in place to ensure that budget units stay within the limits of their authorization. The budget must be kept on track, because many impediments can derail implementation.

Accounting software helps in this regard. It detects quantitative deviations from budgeted revenues and expenditures. In that way, it is the primary tool used to control revenues and expenditures. Nevertheless, humans must play a role, for accounting software may not detect revenue-generating activities or expenditures that deviate from those implicit in the strategic plan. On the revenue side, to raise cash a department might undertake activities unrelated to its mission. Similarly, on the expenditure side, a department might spend on items unrelated to its mission. For example, a college of agriculture may operate a for-profit internet service to help nearby rural communities and then spend the net revenue on activities benefiting students. Despite its beneficial social impact, this activity deviates from the college's strategic plan; it is not encompassed within the college's mission. To control deviations like this, people must be involved, judgments must be made. Should the college be allowed to operate this service anyway? Fiscal officers perform this aspect of control manually as they review transactions. The point is that accounting software is an important element of the control process but it does not replace humans entirely.

Variances

The difference between the amounts of revenue and expenditures authorized in the budget and the actual amounts generated or spent is called the *variance*. Universities monitor variances in all budget units throughout the fiscal year, comparing budgeted and actual revenues and expenditures. Accounting software, of course, calculates variances automatically in real time. Most universities issue analytical reports documenting variances to the budget units at least two, and often four, times each year. These are known as *variance reports*, and they constitute the primary source of metrics for evaluating performance in the budgetary context. As Stanford University notes: "Periodically through the year, as determined by University management, budget officers provide analysis and explanation of the variance between actual income and expense (or projected income and expense) and the Consolidated Budget in accordance with the guidelines provided by the University Budget Office."[1]

These budget variance reports play an important role in maintaining financial stability. By alerting administrators about any deviations between the budgeted and actual expenditures, they highlight any needed financial or managerial adjustments. In other words, they inform department chairs, deans, and the provost about whether their budget unit is keeping to the plan. Final variance reports issued at the end of the fiscal year will be discussed in the context of budget closure in chapter 7.

Variance reports assume that the budget tracks linearly throughout the fiscal year, along a straight line. What does that mean? By assumption, the revenue in the original budget comes into the university at a uniform rate one day at a time. Accordingly, at the end of the first quarter, one-fourth of the year's revenue has been recorded; at midyear, one-half of the year's revenue has been recorded, and so forth until the end of the year, when all of the revenue for the year has been recorded. Likewise, by assumption, the expenditures authorized in the original budget are spent at a uniform rate one day at a time: at the end of the first quarter, one-fourth of the expenditures has been recorded, and so forth throughout the year. Whenever a variance report is prepared on a specific day during the year, the year-to-date (YTD) revenue and expenditures are calculated based on the number of days that have elapsed since the beginning of the fiscal year. For example, at midyear, the YTD budget expenditures are assumed to be half of the original budget expenditures. In the variance report, the actual expenditures are compared with these calculated YTD budget expenditures. Some universities also compare YTD actual expenditures with the original budget projected expenditures.

Technically, the usual (but not universal) convention for reporting variances for both revenue and expenditures is

Variance = Actual − Budgeted.

Often the variances are reported as percentages. By convention,

$$\text{Variance \%} = \frac{\text{Actual} - \text{Budgeted}}{\text{Budgeted}} \times 100 = \frac{\text{Variance}}{\text{Budgeted}} \times 100.$$

Also by convention, a variance is considered *favorable* when the actual revenue is more than the budgeted revenue or when the actual expenditures are less than the budgeted expenditures. Vice versa, a variance is considered *unfavorable* when the actual revenue is less than the budgeted revenue or when the actual expenditures are more than the budgeted expenditures. By this convention, favorable revenue variances are positive and favorable expenditure variances are negative. In budget shorthand, the descriptors "favorable" and "unfavorable" are denoted simply by F or U, respectively. These relationships are summarized in table 6.1.

Ideally, variances are zero: revenues equal expenditures. The budget is balanced, manifesting competent budget forecasts and management. Realistically, of course, deviations from zero are expected. Some deviations may be cyclical and therefore predictable. Tuition revenue, for example, is expected to spike at the

TABLE 6.1. *Variance classifications*

Budget item	Variance	Value	Classification	Symbol
Revenue	Actual > projected	Positive	Favorable	F
	Actual = projected	Zero	Balanced	
	Actual < projected	Negative	Unfavorable	U
Expenditures	Actual > projected	Positive	Unfavorable	U
	Actual = projected	Zero	Balanced	
	Actual < projected	Negative	Favorable	F

beginning of each semester and then drop to nearly zero for the remainder of the semester. Other deviations may be less predictable. For example, personnel come and go during the year, with attendant changes in salary expenditures; the costs of supplies, repairs, maintenance, and various other expenses go up and down, depending on circumstances. Unpredictable deviations generally draw attention and may require an explanation to the next-higher budget officer in the hierarchy. As an expedient, universities may impose a threshold for detailed explanations of a variance from the budget unit director. For example, according to Stanford University's policy, "An explanation is required if a variance exceeds the greater of ±$500,000 or ±10%."[2]

A sample midyear variance report for the department budget (table 2.1) is shown in table 6.2. The variance report was issued at the beginning of the second half of FY 2020, January 1, 2020, so it reports actual expenditures for the first half of FY 2020, from the beginning of the fiscal year, July 1, 2019, to halfway through the fiscal year, December 31, 2019. Assuming a straight-line budget, the YTD budgeted amounts were assumed to be one-half of the original budgeted amount. That is, budgeted revenue and expenditure amounts were assumed to be equal in the first and second halves of FY 2020. In this example, encumbrances are included in the actual expenditure amounts, although some universities break out the encumbrances and list them in a separate column since the encumbered cash has not yet been spent.

The variances (amounts and percentages) are reported relative to the YTD budget and are denoted as favorable (F) or unfavorable (U). The only favorable variance is for the graduate assistant item, where the department spent $5,000 less than budgeted:

Variance (YTD Actual − YTD Budget) = $15,000 − $20,000 = −$5,000.

Remember that although the variance is negative, it is favorable in this case because less money has been spent than budgeted.

TABLE 6.2. *Department budget midyear variance report*

| | 2020 budget | YTD (January 1, 2020) | | Variance: YTD actual − YTD budget | |
		Budget	Actual	Amount	%
Revenue allocation	1,000,000	500,000	500,000		
Expenditures					
Salaries					
Faculty	700,000	350,000	350,000		
Professional					
Administrative	100,000	50,000	50,000		
Classified employee					
Graduate assistant	40,000	20,000	15,000	(5,000)F	−25.00
Faculty summer salary					
Student wages	8,000	4,000	5,000	1,000U	25.00
Other compensation	2,000	1,000	2,000	1,000U	100.00
Termination payouts					
Subtotal salaries	850,000	425,000	422,000	(3,000)F	−0.71
Operations					
Contracted services	12,000	6,000	6,000		
Supplies and materials	10,000	5,000	6,000	1,000U	20.00
Communications	4,000	2,000	2,000		
Travel	10,000	5,000	8,000	3,000U	60.00
Rent					
Utilities					
Repairs and maintenance	1,000	500	1,000	500U	100.00
Other	13,000	6,500	12,000	5,500U	84.62
Subtotal operations	50,000	25,000	35,000	10,000U	40.00
Scholarships	100,000	50,000	50,000		
Total expenditures	1,000,000	500,000	507,000	7,000U	1.40

Note: See table 6.1 for definition of letter symbols.

That $5,000 surplus should be available for graduate assistant support in the second half of the fiscal year. All of the other variances are unfavorable because the department overspent in the first half of the year. Clearly, the chair must reduce the spending rate for student wages, other compensation, supplies, and travel. Hypothetically, the "Other" operations expenditure line item included a $6,000 piece of equipment, such as a copy machine, that the department bought early in the fiscal year. Therefore, that unfavorable variance ($5,500) is less worrisome.

Some universities also report YTD variances relative to the original budget. These variances indicate the amount of money available for specific line items during the remainder of the fiscal year. That information is useful but potentially misleading. For example, in table 6.2 on January 1, 2020 (mid-year), the department has spent $5,000 on student wages, leaving $3,000 for the remainder of the year:

Variance (YTD Actual – Original Budget) = $5,000 – $8,000 = –$3,000.

The variance is favorable, because there is still $3,000 remaining for the rest of the year. But this is $2,000 less than it spent for student wages in the first half of the year ($5,000), which is manifest as an unfavorable variance relative to the YTD budget. Similarly, the department has $2,000 remaining for travel (a favorable variance), but that is $6,000 less than it spent in the first half of the year (an unfavorable YTD variance). As in these two examples, favorable variances relative to the original budget could be misleading and must be examined carefully if the variances relative to the YTD budget are unfavorable. On the one hand, there may have been careless spending during the first half of the year, which must be corrected in the second half of the year. On the other hand, there may be reasonable explanations. For example, most scholarly conferences occur during the fall, so the travel budget is spent predominantly in the first half of the year.

Budget Modifications

During the fiscal year, variances may trigger budget modifications designed to mitigate the variance. These in-year modifications constitute an important means of budget control. Their impact depends on the locus of the variance. If the variance occurs at the institutional level, modifications of the master budget affect budget units throughout the hierarchy. If the variance is in specific line items at the department level, modifications seldom extend beyond the individual department.

The procedures for mitigating variances through in-year budget modifications vary depending on the locus of the variance and the budget model's flexibility.

Revised Budgets

Using updated information, the CFO may revise institutional revenue or expenditure projections at least once during the fiscal year to account for significant changes from the original master budget. Revised projections generally follow changes in budget items that affect the entire university, such as state appropriations or allocations, tuition and fee income, and any other sources of institutional revenue or unanticipated major expenditures. Consequent to these revisions, the CFO issues a *revised budget*. Operating budgets usually are revised at least once during the fiscal year to account for changes in state appropriations or allocations, updated tuition and fee income, and any other sources of revenue or anticipated major expenditures.

Conceivably, the revised budget may reflect increased revenue, with implicit opportunities to increase expenditures. An unanticipated windfall of funds is rare, but most CFOs will know in advance how to deploy additional resources as soon as they are identified. They have a prioritized list of items not in the budget to fund if resources become available—either through a windfall or through unanticipated savings. As a result, most budget units may not benefit directly from the opportunity to increase expenditures, because the CFO may choose not to distribute the additional revenue to budget units lower in the hierarchy. Instead, the CFO may retain unanticipated revenue for institutional unbudgeted expenditures, such as transfers into a reserve account or, more likely than not, repairs of deferred maintenance items.

In contrast, the revised budget may reflect decreased revenue, conveying an explicit need to decrease expenditures. A revenue shortfall triggers revisions to the operating budgets throughout the hierarchy. In a sense, the operating budget must be reconstructed to account for the revisions.

Irrespective of whether revenues increased or decreased, the revision process recapitulates the steps in phase two of the budget cycle (figure 5.1). As in the original budget process (chapter 5), the revised budget process begins when the CFO issues revised revenue projections. Also as in the original budget process, in the next step, the provost issues revenue allocations, based on the revised revenue projections, to the budget units lower in the hierarchy. However, the procedure for allocating the original and the revised revenue allocations diverge at this point.

The divergence occurs because reducing authorized expenditures in response to a budget revision is tantamount to taking back money. Funds are recaptured, not to establish a contingency fund but to rebalance expenditures with revenues. This taking back goes by several names, including *rescission*, proration, reversion, and claw-back. They all mean the same thing: returning a portion of the originally budgeted authorization. For everybody concerned, this is an unpleasant experience.

Rescissions may be across the board or program specific. That distinction can be made at each level of the hierarchy. Hypothetically, the state budget office, the governing board, or the CFO determines how much must be taken back to rebalance the consolidated budget. The president, in consultation with the provost and the CFO, then decides whether to distribute the rescissions proportionately across the board to the entire campus (academic affairs, physical plant, finance and administration, and so forth) or disproportionately to specific units (such as academic affairs). Regardless, rescission instructions for academic affairs go to the provost. The provost also must then decide whether to assess rescissions across the board, proportionately to each dean, or to specific colleges disproportionately. Likewise, the deans must make similar decisions regarding the departments under their authority.

Theoretically, across-the-board rescissions are easy to administer. For example, every budget unit must return 3 percent of its authorized expenditures to the next-higher level. Realistically, however, administering them can be difficult. Some departments may not be able to accommodate their rescissions without adverse instructional consequences—for example, they may need to lay off teaching personnel, including nontenured faculty members, or reduce the number of graduate teaching and research assistants. Anecdotally, after the announcement of a 4 percent rescission because of reduced state appropriations, a medical school dean told the provost, "We can no longer to offer the M.D. degree." Pronouncements like that are hard to ignore. These and other imaginable stumbling blocks can make simple across-the-board rescissions very complicated.

Nonetheless, selective disproportional rescissions can be even more difficult to administer. The major challenge resides in deciding how to levy the rescissions. Which budget units receive disproportionately large rescission targets and, conversely, which budget units receive disproportionately small rescission targets? This challenge confronts each budget unit in the hierarchy: the CFO, the provost, and the deans. In principle, the decisions should be consistent with the strategic plan. As a best practice, they should be made in consultation with budget advisory groups at each level in the hierarchy. This practice enlists the wisdom of the group and, perhaps more important, generates buy-in. Furthermore, such consultation makes the decision easier to defend when disgruntled recipients of disproportion-ately large rescission targets express their displeasure.

Notwithstanding the actual allocation process, after receiving their revised allocations, the budget units prepare revised budgets. At this step, the revised and the original budget processes converge, as the revised budgets flow up to the provost, who prepares the revised academic operating budget. Ultimately, the CFO assembles the revised consolidated university budget.

A sample revised consolidated budget for fiscal year 2020 is shown in table 6.3. The 2020 original budget (table 2.2) was revised following a $2 million decrease in revenue (−2.20 percent), due mainly to a $2 million decrease in state appropriations relative to original projections. The revised revenue and expenditure projections ($88,900,000) were distributed to budget units lower in the hierarchy, and they prepared revised budgets based on the revised expenditures authorized by the provost and the deans. On consolidation of their revised budgets, the total authorized expenditures were decreased by $2 million, thus rebalancing the consolidated budget. Not surprisingly, the largest percentage decrease in expenditures (−14.29 percent) was in the operations line (−$700,000), as the budget units tried to protect the salary and fringe benefits lines.

Budget Adjustments

Throughout the year, budgets are adjusted routinely to mitigate variances. Accordingly, budget accounting software may have built-in controls blocking transactions that contribute to an unfavorable variance. For blocked transactions to proceed, some financial remedy is needed: the budget must be adjusted to add more revenue or to curb expenditures.

The ease of making these in-year budget adjustments depends on the budget's flexibility. For the most part, university operating budgets are inherently static, as described in chapter 3. They are not designed to change over the course of the fiscal year. In fact, variance analysis is predicated on a static budget. Therefore,

TABLE 6.3. *Revised consolidated budget for 2020*

	2020 original	2020 revised	Change	
			Amount	%
Revenues				
Tuition	20,000,000	20,000,000		
Student fees	500,000	500,000		
State appropriations	51,000,000	49,000,000	(2,000,000)	−3.92
Grants and contracts	7,000,000	7,000,000		
Auxiliary	11,000,000	10,900,000	(100,000)	−0.91
Outreach	1,400,000	1,500,000	100,000	7.14
Total	90,900,000	88,900,000	(2,000,000)	−2.20
Expenditures				
Salaries and wages	63,000,000	62,000,000	(1,000,000)	−1.59
Fringe benefits	21,000,000	20,700,000	(300,000)	−1.43
Operations	4,900,000	4,200,000	(700,000)	−14.29
Scholarships	2,000,000	2,000,000		
Total	90,900,000	88,900,000	(2,000,000)	−2.20

within a rigidly static budget model, in-year budget adjustments are limited to best- or worst-case scenarios. At best, the budget unit can draw upon contingency or unrestricted reserve funds to supplement inadequate revenues. After all, that is the purpose of rainy-day funds. This desirable strategy buffers the impact of reduced revenue or overspending on programmatic activities. At worst, planned expenditures must be reduced (for example, travel is curtailed, new hiring is frozen, pay raises are deferred). This undesirable but potentially unavoidable strategy disrupts scheduled programmatic activities unless they can be reduced in an orderly fashion. In the most malignant situations, commitments cannot be honored. Purchase orders and work contracts are canceled, job offers are rescinded, and repairs and maintenance are deferred. Of course, universities try to avoid these situations.

Within the constraints of a static budget model, however, most universities allow some flexibility to facilitate necessary in-year budget adjustments to correct unfavorable variances.

Budget Transfers

The easiest adjustment involves *budget transfers*. This common, relatively benign adjustment to correct unfavorable variances involves transferring funds from one budget category (account) to another. For example, expenditure authorization is shifted from one account with a favorable variance to another with an unfavorable variance. This adjustment constitutes a budget transfer. In budget-transfer accounting, the "from" refers to a credit which reduces the balance of the donor account and the "to" refers to a debit which increases the balance of the receiving account.

Although universities routinely allow budget transfers, they often impose limitations on them. Fundamentally, the transfers should not change the strategic goals expressed in the budget. That is, they should not change the scope and intentions of the authorized expenditures in the original budget. Therefore, transfers from one budget category to another generally require higher-level approval to ensure consistency with the original budget. As an administrative expedient, higher-level approvals may be waived if the transfers are less than a specific threshold (such as $5,000). Furthermore, fundamentally, the transfers should not affect other budget units or all-campus priorities. That is, their impact must be confined to the budget unit making the transfer. Therefore, regardless of the amount, transfers usually require higher-level approval if they involve items such as student financial aid, debt service, the physical plant, required reserve contributions, and similar items. Of course, all transfers must be balanced. That is, the money taken from one category must equal the money entered into another category.

Typically, the unit's budget officer processes transfers through the budget accounting software, which has built-in controls (entered by the central budget office) that block any unauthorized transfers. Procedurally, when blocking a transaction, the software issues a notification to both the budget unit and the higher-level authority. Approval by the higher-level authority, allowing the failed transaction to pass, may depend on a persuasive justification prepared by the budget unit. A wise budgeter will have prepared a justification in advance.

A hypothetical budget modification form, generated by accounting software, is shown in table 6.4. After the department fiscal officer logged in and entered a description of the transaction and the account numbers involved in the transfer, the software automatically assigned a reference number to the transaction, filled in the fund number, department identification number (ID), and current balance (original budget). The fiscal officer then entered the transaction: transfer $1,000 from one account (51000) to another (58000). The software automatically coded the two separate entries as a decrease or increase and a credit or debit as well as the new account balances (adjusted budget). It's done. Of course, transactions can become much more complicated, but as this example shows, the software eases the entire transaction process.

Incidentally, favorable variances also may require budget adjustments. For example, to spend unanticipated revenue, which results in a favorable variance, the expenditure component of the budget must be modified. The new revenue must be assigned to some expenditure, thus increasing some account balances. Again, these modifications must conform to the original budget's strategic intent. Therefore, transfers of additional revenue into an expenditure category generally are subject to the same limitations as unfavorable variances, with higher-level approval required if they exceed specific threshold amounts or have an impact beyond the budget unit.

TABLE 6.4. *Budget modification form*

Unit name:	Chemistry				Reference number: 82813		
Requested By:	dos				Request date: 06/21/2018		
Description:	Add to student recruitment travel account						

Account	Fund	Department ID	Original budget	Adjustment balance	Decrease/ increase	Adjusted balance	Credit/ debit
51000	21	203	*$6,000.00*	$1,000.00	*Decrease*	*$5,000.00*	*Credit*
58000	21	203	*$1,000.00*	$1,000.00	*Increase*	*$2,000.00*	*Debit*

Note: Fields in italics are filled in automatically.

Structural Surpluses and Deficits

Structural surpluses occur when ongoing revenues exceed expenditures for two or more fiscal years. A priori, this welcome situation appears easy to manage. Give everybody more money. But that would be foolish unless the additional money were spent concordant with the strategic plan. Wise use of the money entails reevaluating the budget's relationship to the strategic plan. Questions arise. Is the strategic plan overly cautious? Should the plan add new priorities or enhance investment in current priorities? Should the university look to the future by investing additional revenues in quasi-endowments and paying down debt? And so forth. The important point is this: sensible use of structural surpluses requires thoughtful deliberation.

Conversely, structural deficits occur when universities confront periods of chronic budgetary stress, with expenditures exceeding revenues for two or more fiscal years. This stress manifests a structural imbalance in the budget that must be managed in ways that do not seriously derail normal operations. It, too, entails re-evaluating the budget's relationship to the strategic plan. Different questions arise. Is the strategic plan realistic? Should it be updated to reflect the current financial and academic environment? Are the strategic goals overly ambitious? And so forth. The answers to these questions also require thoughtful deliberation. Many books on university administration document various strategies guiding these deliberations.

Unfortunately, when confronted initially by structural deficits, universities must either raise additional revenue or decrease expenditures before the thoughtful deliberation process runs its course. Raising additional revenue may require the institution to increase tuition, endowment payout, state appropriations, or debt. Each of these can be difficult to manage in the short term, especially in public universities, where other state agencies compete for state appropriations. Often the public response to the university's plea for increased appropriations to cure structural deficits is simply a call to reduce expenditures by increasing efficiencies. And the belt-tightening begins. In contrast, decreasing expenditures can be accomplished quickly by freezing hiring, deferring building and grounds maintenance, and reducing library acquisitions, among other steps. Unfortunately, these measures are not sustainable. Hiring freezes are particularly pernicious because of the random occurrence of faculty vacancies. Longer-term solutions must be found.

Budget Cuts

A routine long-term solution to structural deficits is budget cutting, sometimes called *retrenchment*, either across the board or selectively. Neither is easy to accomplish without rancor. Across-the-board cuts are generally unpopular, especially among the academic units (colleges and departments) that consider themselves among those favored in the strategic plan or ranked highly in national rankings. And selective cuts, like selective rescissions, are generally even more difficult to make because they require programmatic decisions to be made, usually with extensive faculty involvement. That is always challenging in a university environment.

Ironically, when budgets must be cut, restricted funds may become more valuable than unrestricted funds because they are immune to cuts. As NACUBO puts it: "Although most money is 'green,' restricted funds may have the effect of allowing budget owners in those areas to escape the competitive fray for resources that other programs without restricted funds must enter. This does not necessarily enable an institution to maximize its resources."[3] An example illustrates this point. Imagine a college of arts and sciences and a college of engineering, each of which has a $10,000,000 operating budget. Restricted funds constitute 25 and 50 percent, respectively, of their budgets. Thus, the unrestricted components of the arts and sciences and the engineering budgets are $7,500,000 and $5,000,000, respectively. A 10 percent cut in general funds must come out of their unrestricted budget component. Consequently, the budget cut in the college of arts and sciences, $750,000, is $250,000 more than the cut in the college of engineering, $500,000. Clearly, engineering has a distinct advantage when budget cuts occur because of its greater percentage of restricted funds.

Significantly, in this example budgets were cut across the board. To equalize the impact of budget cuts, the engineering budget would have to be cut more than the arts and sciences budget, resulting in a selective budget cut. If this were to occur, the college of engineering would protest vigorously: "Why punish us because we successfully raised outside money?" Unfortunately for engineering, NACUBO counsels that "financial officers have a mandate to responsibly link mission, strategy, budgets, and assessment, without allowing their thinking to become confused by the changing exigencies of funding source."[4]

Consolidations and Closures

In the most severe structural budget crises, the governing board usually calls for *downsizing*, which is code for laying off personnel and terminating academic units. When this occurs, universities must consider consolidating or eliminating programs (for example, a department or a specific degree) to reduce overall expenditures. The usual process involves analyses of various cost objects within the university (departments, degree programs, athletic teams, and so forth) in the context of the strategic plan by committees comprising mainly faculty members but also including staff and student representatives. Particular attention focuses on programs with declining enrollment, accreditation problems, or low academic productivity (in terms of publications, grants, or doctoral degrees awarded). These are not easy analyses, because they set faculty members against each other. Faculty unions are particularly sensitive to this issue. Furthermore, faculty members are far more comfortable with additive than with subtractive allocations because they are constructive, not destructive. Anything beyond that additive comfort zone lies outside the acceptable limits of their shared authority.[5] Nonetheless, decisions must be made, and specific programs must be designated for consolidation or closure.

As most administrators and governing board members in this situation have discovered, consolidating or closing programs can be devilishly difficult if not impossible. Every academic program seems to have its protective constituents, and one way or another they can exert strong pressure to maintain the status quo, regardless of budgetary implications. Ultimately, however, the process must go forward if operational costs are to be reduced.

Pragmatically, program closure is phased over several years. In the case of a department closure, for example, the standard first step is to stop admitting new students into the department. Students in the pipeline must be accommodated, which usually means that they remain enrolled in the department until they finish their program of study. As a result, the department must continue to teach relevant courses until the students finish. Similarly, sponsored projects must be brought to an orderly conclusion: experiments completed, manuscripts written, reports filed. Furthermore, personnel contracts must be honored. Nontenure-track employees must be allowed to complete the terms of their contract, which may extend up to three years. Tenured faculty members must be transferred to another department unless the university decides to declare a *financial exigency*, which is tantamount to setting aside tenure. Regardless, these arrangements also take time. Therefore, the full cost savings from the phased closure may not be recognized for several years.

A hypothetical anecdote further illustrates the phase-out process. For the past several years, the astronomy department has spent a lot more than it brought in. This overspending has been a recurrent problem, so the governing board directed the president to close the department. The closure will be phased over a five-year period starting in 2020. In the first year, no more students are admitted to the department, leading to a 25 percent reduction in tuition revenue. As students complete their programs over the next three years, tuition revenue continues to decline. As their three-year contracts expire, nontenured faculty members are laid off at a rate of 25 percent per year, thus reducing expenditures accordingly. The number of sponsored projects also declines as nontenured faculty members are laid off. Likewise, as the number of personnel declines, the operating budget (supplies and services) declines by 25 percent a year. By 2023, only tenured faculty members remain in the department, with their sponsored project revenue and salary and fringe benefit expenses. In 2024, these tenured faculty members are transferred to another department, along with their sponsored project revenue and salary and fringe benefit costs, concluding the phase-out. The department is now closed. Notably, the university does not recognize positive fund balances until the second year of the phase-out (2021). Moreover, the ultimate savings is only a fraction of the total expenditures in 2019, owing to the tuition and grant revenue lost because of the closure. Typically, the fraction saved is about 40 to 50 percent of the total expenditures before the beginning of the closure process.[6]

These calculations assume that all personnel are taken off the department's payroll. For soft-money research appointments supported by sponsored grants and contracts, this is doable. But faculty members, especially those with tenure, will resist dismissal, and, as in the anecdote, the university may end up reassigning some or all of them to faculty positions in other departments. Any litigation in this context will consume time and legal fees. This and other imaginable scenarios can seriously erode the actual net savings from departmental closure to the point where the question arises: Is it worth all of this?

As shown in this chapter, implementation of the budget can be challenging, requiring constant attention. However, as time passes, the fiscal year comes to an end and attention turns to implementation of a new budget. This transition from one fiscal year to the next raises a new flurry of activity, which is the topic of the next chapter.

Chapter 7

End of the Fiscal Year

W hen the fiscal year comes to an end, the budget also comes to an end, as authorization to add revenue or initiate expenditures expires. The only residual authority pertains to encumbrances not yet liquidated, and those must be paid within a short, specified period of time before that authority expires also. From this period in time onward, the past year's budget becomes just that: a thing of the past. The financial officers' attention turns to closing the books on the past year's financial activities in preparation for the new fiscal year.

The process of closing the fiscal year that affects budget units most directly spans nearly a two-month period encompassing basically the last month of the current fiscal year and the first month of the next fiscal year when adjustments are made. Many other things happen during this time period. The new fiscal year budget must be launched: new accounts must be set up and personnel must be appointed, among other things. On the surface, closing the fiscal year engenders an atmosphere of controlled chaos, where financial administration may look out of control but actually functions according to well-established practices. Those practices are the topic of this chapter.

Closing the Budget

By definition, *closing the budget* means that no further revenue can be added and no further expenditures can be charged to the budget. Closing the budget derives from the accounting premise that expenditures should be paid during the fiscal year when the benefits from the expenditures are received. Procedurally, a budget can be closed only after its end date, the fiscal year, has passed. This implies that closure occurs only after a budget for the next fiscal year has been prepared. Furthermore, closure is irreversible; a closed budget cannot be reopened.

To smooth the transition from one budget to the next, universities set deadlines for various transactions during the closing process. The rationale is to allow sufficient time to liquidate (pay) encumbrances before the end of the fiscal year. A sample timeline with significant deadlines and events for the current fiscal year (which ends on June 30) is shown in table 7.1. Each of the listed transactions must be submitted to the fiscal office by the deadline date to be charged to the current year's budget. After the deadlines, these expenditures can no longer be charged to the current year's budget.

Usually, the earliest deadline applies to payroll forms. In the example, payroll forms for new employees must be received by June 4 (day number 1 on the timeline) in order to be paid from the current year's budget on June 30. The early deadline occurs because payroll transactions undergo an extensive, multi-office review. The review process may vary depending on the institution and type of employee. Typically, after a new payroll transaction is initiated by the department and approved by the dean and perhaps the provost, the college budget office determines funding availability. Then the human resources office reviews compliance with institutional policies, including affirmative action. Finally, the transaction goes to payroll for final review and processing. Frequently, corrections must be made along the way. All of this takes time.

TABLE 7.1. *Fiscal year closing timeline*

Day number	Deadline date	Transactions and *significant events*
1	4-June	Payroll forms
19	22-June	New purchase orders
26	29-June	University store purchases
27	30-June	Revenue deposits
27	*30-June*	*Current fiscal year ends*
28	*1-July*	*New fiscal year begins*
32	5-July	Purchase order invoices
38	11-July	Journal entries
39	12-July	Budget transfers
53	*26-July*	*Pre-audit closing*

Note: To be charged to the current year's budget, the transactions listed must be completed by the deadline date.

In contrast, purchase orders (POs) for goods and services must be issued by a later date, June 22. The later deadline occurs because administering POs is relatively simple. The purchasing software system checks fund availability when the requisition is entered. Then the only other review is by a fiscal officer in the purchasing office. Unless there are unanticipated complications, the PO can be issued within a few days. In fact, most universities have an expedited process if time is short. The deadline for purchases made from in-house stores operated by the university can be even later (June 29), because their billing systems are linked directly to the university's accounting software system.

The deadline for depositing revenue is usually much closer to the end of the fiscal year. Indeed, in this example, it is the close of business on the last day of the fiscal year (June 30). This timing is possible because electronic systems greatly speed up banking processes. In this case, therefore, checks, cash, credit card receipts, and so forth may be deposited in the university's treasury account on June 30 to be debited to that fiscal year's budget.

Sometimes purchases or a payment are made in one fiscal year for goods or services that must be accounted for in the next fiscal year. Examples include travel and registration fees for a conference in the next fiscal year, rent paid in advance, subscriptions for the next fiscal year, and payments for software licenses for the next year. Those expenses are recorded in so-called prepaid accounts and are transferred as expenditures to the appropriate account as the goods and services are received in the new fiscal year. They do not affect the current year's budget.

Ideally, at the end of the fiscal year, all encumbrances would have been liquidated (paid) and outstanding revenue inflows would have been deposited. The transition from this year's budget to next year's budget would occur smoothly, with no overlap. In reality, this seldom occurs. At year's end, an ordered good has not yet been delivered; the invoice for a delivered good has not arrived and been paid; checks are received but cannot be deposited at the last minute. To improve the chances of an orderly transition from one fiscal year to the next, universities may extend the deadlines for deliveries, invoice payments, and last-minute deposits into the next fiscal year, backdating them to the previous fiscal year. But the extensions are short, only several days, because keeping two budgets open at the same time can become chaotic. In the example shown in table 7.1, the university extends the invoice payment window five days into the new fiscal year, to July 5.

After these deadlines have passed, there are two approaches for handling unliquidated encumbrances. In the more common approach, universities roll them forward to the new budget. The advantage is that the purchase order remains open, awaiting delivery and invoicing. The disadvantage is that the encumbrance must be paid using funds from the new budget, which cuts into the amount available for the new fiscal year's planned expenditures. Alternatively, universities cancel all outstanding purchase orders if the goods and services are not received and paid for by the end of the fiscal year. This strict policy requires closer attention to manage the budget properly. The advantage is that no lingering commitments extend beyond the end of the fiscal year. The new budget starts with a clean slate. The disadvantage is that purchase orders must be rewritten in the new fiscal year, which is likely to delay delivery of the goods or services. Because of the increased effort required and the potentially disruptive delays, this alternative method is less commonly used.

As the closing period winds down, the accounting staff reviews (*scrubs*) the past year's budget to ensure its accuracy. Any necessary adjustments are made through journal entries and budget transfers that are backdated to June 30. In the example, these adjustments must be completed by July 11 and July 12, respectively. These are the last major accounting activities affecting the past fiscal year's budget.

During the remaining two weeks or so, the university's financial accountants are *closing the books* for the fiscal year. The phrase "closing the books" means that all revenue and expense accounts are closed with a zero balance at the end of the fiscal year. That is, they are "zeroed out" in preparation for the new fiscal year. This is done by transferring account balances. Positive net balances go to net asset accounts. Then, the CFO's office prepares a trial balance as the starting point for an independent financial audit. At that time, further accounting entries are frozen until the audit is complete. This step is called the *pre-audit closing* (July 26). At the conclusion of the audit, any adjusting entries are made. The final closure occurs several weeks later. At that time, the books are closed.

Financial Statements

After closing the books, the university prepares its annual *financial statements*, which "tell the story of the revenues and expenses that materialized during the year."[1] They summarize the organization's financial status in three separate documents:

- balance sheet
- income statement
- statement of cash flows

Together, the financial statements report the university's net worth, net revenue earned, and cash inflow and outflow, respectively. In addition, details about these financial statements—calculation methods, itemization, unusual circumstances, and other pertinent explanations—are documented in accompanying footnotes. These notes are an important component of the financial statements.

All publicly traded, government, and nonprofit organizations must include financial statements in their financial reports. The financial statements are meant to present financial information as clearly and concisely as possible for audiences both external and internal to the organization. In the for-profit sector, the primary audience is the shareholders, whereas in the nonprofit sector, the primary audiences are the governing board, legislators, investors, and donors. To standardize this information, two different organizations, the Financial Accounting Standards Board (FASB) and the Government Accounting Standards Board (GASB), have established guidelines that private and public universities, respectively, must adhere to when preparing their financial statements. Although the formats and names of the FASB and GASB financial statements differ somewhat, their fundamental content does not differ significantly.

Unlike budgets, which are based on revenue and expenditure *projection*s, financial statements are based on *actual* revenue and expenditure data. Budgets look forward; financial statements look backward. As a result, the financial statements provide a different view of the university's financial performance. This section will briefly introduce financial statements and compare them with budgets. More details are available in *University Finances: Accounting and Budgeting Principles for Higher Education*.[2]

Balance Sheet

The balance sheet, referred to as the *statement of financial position* and the *statement of net position* by private and public universities, respectively, provides information about the institution's worth at a specific point in time, generally the last day of the fiscal year. Although the format and nomenclature for public and private universities differ slightly, basically their balance sheets report the total assets, liabilities, and net assets according to the fundamental accounting equation:

Assets = Liabilities + Net Assets.

Obviously, the balance sheet always must be in balance. This follows the same principle of double-entry accounting that governs the general ledger. However, instead of showing individual accounting transactions, as in the general ledger, the balance sheet presents a snapshot summarizing the institution's accounts at the end of the fiscal year.

When evaluating the university's overall financial status, the balance sheet is particularly useful. It answers questions such as: How much cash does the university have on hand? How much long-term debt does the university owe? Answers to questions like these provide insight into the overall financial context of the budget. For example, if the university has little cash, the CFO may be inclined to allocate some revenue to a cash reserve account instead of to academic programs.

The balance sheet is of limited use, however, when evaluating budget performance. Comparisons between the budget and the balance sheet are difficult because they use different accounting bases. The budget uses the cash basis, which recognizes revenue when cash is received and expenses when bills are paid. However, the balance sheet uses the accrual basis, which recognizes (records) revenue when it is earned and expenses when they are incurred, whether or not any cash is received or paid. Furthermore, unlike the budget, the balance sheet does not provide information about financial activities during the year. Fortunately, the next two financial statements are more useful in that regard.

Income Statement

The income statement, called the *statement of activities* and the *statement of revenues, expenses, and changes in net position* by private and public universities, respectively, illustrates the financial viability of an organization. It provides information that explains how assets, liabilities, and net assets change with time. Unlike the balance sheet, which focuses on assets and liabilities, the income statement focuses on revenues and expenses and how they affect net assets. And unlike the balance sheet's one-day time frame, the income statement covers a longer time frame such as a fiscal year. Overall, it presents financial information about an institution's operating activities, investments, and fundraising during the reporting period.

Accordingly, a university's income statement reports the amount of revenue earned over a specific time frame, usually a fiscal year, as well as the expenses directly related to earning that revenue. Revenue minus expenses yields the change in net assets during the fiscal year; in equation form, it can be written as

Change in Net Assets = Revenue – Expenses.

Noticeably, this equation resembles the corresponding equation for the budget's fund balance:

Change in Fund Balance = Revenue – Expenditures.

As this resemblance in the equations suggests, the income statement looks like the university's master budget. Indeed, the income statement is a measure of institutional operations, much like the budget. They both report revenue and expenses in about the same categories. Significantly, the income statement summarizes the actual revenues and expenditures of the past fiscal year. In that respect, the income statement and the budget resemble each other even more.

Because of its resemblance to the budget, the income statement can be useful when evaluating the past year's budget performance. However, this usefulness is limited. The resemblance of the income statement and the budget might imply that the corresponding revenue and expenditure amounts are the same in both documents. This may in fact occur in some entries, but more often than not corresponding amounts differ. These discrepancies manifest the fundamental difference between a budget and a financial statement: like the balance sheet, the income statement is based on accrual accounting, whereas the budget is based on cash accounting.

To be sure, the income statement can be converted to the cash basis. The conversion requires certain revenue and expense reclassifications, transfers, and adjustments to the budget, such as removing capital equipment purchases and recording the current year's depreciation. In fact, that is what happens in the third financial statement, the statement of cash flows.

Statement of Cash Flows

Stated formally, the statement of cash flows provides information about an institution's cash receipts and payments during a specific period, usually the fiscal year. It highlights the net increase and decrease in total cash on hand for the accounting period, indicating actual cash received or spent. In this context, cash includes currency and bank deposits as well as cash equivalents such as highly liquid U.S. Treasury bills, money market accounts, and commercial paper. Other less liquid investments such as stocks and bonds are not considered cash equivalents.

As its name implies, the statement of cash flows uses the cash accounting basis. Thus, it resembles the budget more closely than the other two financial statements, which use the accrual accounting basis. To understand this assertion, it helps to remember that the income statement reports revenues as they are earned and expenses as they are incurred, whether or not cash has been received or paid. In that sense, the income statement provides a full accounting of the university's revenues and expenses. However, because it does not account for the timing of cash exchanges, the accrual method masks the flow of actual cash into and out of the university, leaving unanswered questions about the amount of ready cash available to pay bills. For example, on the income statement, the institution might report substantial revenue. But if the revenue is primarily in accounts receivable and not cash on hand, the university might not be able to pay its bills if the receivables cannot be collected in a timely way.

To unmask the true flow of cash, the statement of cash flows converts net income reported in the income statement from the accrual basis to the cash basis. It does this by making adjustments (usually subtractions in this case) for noncash items in various accounts. These items include accounts receivable, inventory, prepaid assets, payable liabilities, and unearned revenues. The cash flows statement, like the budget, will not include accounts receivable and so forth because they are not cash. In addition, changes that neither provide nor consume cash are removed. So the income statement may show depreciation as an expense, but depreciation does not require a cash outlay and does not appear on the cash flows statement. Nor does it usually appear in a budget. Likewise, items that increase net assets but are long term in nature are removed from operations and reclassified to financing or investing activities. These include contributions for long-term investments, whether in the form of new funds for endowment or funds to be expended for the acquisition or construction of property, plant, or equipment. In general, cash flows from investing and financing activities are not considered part of ongoing regular operating activities. They still, however, represent cash that can be used to pay bills. Therefore, cash from investing and financing is added to cash flow from operations to arrive at the net change in cash and cash equivalents for the year. After these adjustments have been made, the statement of cash flows bottom line measures short-term viability: Will the university have money available to pay daily operating expenses and short-term debt obligations?

Because they use the same accounting basis, the statement of cash flows and the budget can be reconciled. That is, their numbers can be compared. Both private and public university statements of cash flows report actual revenue from various sources such as tuition and fees, grants and contracts, and auxiliary enterprises as well as expenditures on various items such as salaries, fringe benefits, and scholarships. These reported numbers corroborate the actual revenues and expenditures reported in the past fiscal year's budget. In addition, year-end variances in the budget can be compared with cash flows in the financial statements. As a supplement to the budget, therefore, the statement of cash flows can be useful when analyzing the past year's budget performance.

Year-End Variances

After the budget cycle and the financial statements have been completed, each budget unit analyzes the budget performance of the past year. Questions are asked. Did the budget meet estimates? If not, why not? Are there trends that require attention? These analyses focus on fiscal year-end variance reports identifying budget items that may require attention in the next year's budget. Indeed, budget preparers always look at year-end variances when getting ready for the next year's budget.

Large variances understandably attract the most attention. If they are unfavorable, they may result from unexpected fluctuations in revenue or expenditures, such as those following a major hurricane or the loss of a large grant. However, they may also indicate faulty forecasting or fiscal mismanagement by the budget unit, requiring additional staff training. Deans or department chairs who report sizable unfavorable variances several years in a row risk losing their jobs. Of course, it is better if variances are favorable. If they are too large, however, they are not necessarily desirable. For example, large favorable variances in the expense category represent saved money, but they may indicate the budget unit's underinvestment in its academic programs, signaling academic mismanagement. And they raise questions about how much money the budget unit actually needs, which could portend a reduction in the next year's budget allocation.

A sample year-end variance report for a departmental budget is illustrated in table 7.2. The variances are expressed as a percentage of the original budget issued at the beginning of the fiscal year. Notably, faculty salaries are fixed; they seldom vary. Most other items vary to some extent. The administrative salary expenditures were $20,000 less than budgeted, presumably because of an unfilled vacancy; by inference, the job responsibilities were temporarily assigned to a student, because student wages were $2,000 over the budgeted amount. Likewise, graduate assistant expenditures were $5,000 less than budgeted. Unfavorable variances incurred for supplies, travel, and repairs and maintenance were relatively small in dollar amounts but large in percentages. Presumably, they will require explanations. Fortunately, these unfavorable variances were counterbalanced by large favorable variances in salaries. The overall expenditure variance is favorable (–1.50 percent), resulting in a year-end fund balance of $15,000.

Fund Balances

There are three approaches to managing favorable fund balances. First, in a decentralized approach, fund balances roll forward into the new fiscal year, adding to a cumulative balance from previous years. In this approach, departments control their fund balances, which they can use for nonrecurring expenses. Second, in a centralized approach, fund balances revert to the

TABLE 7.2. *Department budget year-end variance report*

	2020 budget		Variance: actual − original budget	
	Original	Actual	Amount	%
Revenue allocation	1,000,000	1,000,000		
Expenditures				
Salaries				
Faculty	700,000	700,000		
Professional				
Administrative	100,000	80,000	(20,000)F	−20.00
Classified employee				
Graduate assistant	40,000	35,000	(5,000)F	−12.50
Faculty summer salary				
Student wages	8,000	10,000	2,000U	25.00
Other compensation	2,000	2,000		
Termination payouts		5,000	5,000U	
Subtotal salaries	850,000	832,000	(18,000)F	−2.12
Operations				
Contracted services	12,000	12,000		
Supplies and materials	10,000	10,500	500U	5.00
Communications	4,000	4,000		
Travel	10,000	12,000	2,000U	20.00
Rent				
Utilities				
Repairs and maintenance	1,000	1,500	500U	50.00
Other	13,000	13,000		
Subtotal operations	50,000	53,000	3,000U	6.00
Scholarships	100,000	100,000		
Total expenditures	1,000,000	985,000	(15,000)F	−1.50
Fund balance		15,000		

Note: See table 6.1 for definition of letter symbols.

university's general fund, and the budget units lose the ability to allocate and spend the money. This common approach rolls fund balances forward but aggregates them centrally. Naturally, many presidents and CFOs like this approach because they can decide how the funds are expended. Third, in the least common approach, some states do not allow the university to roll fund balances forward. Any unexpended funds revert to the state. In other words, the institution must use it or lose it.

Ultimately, even if departments retain favorable fund balances, as in the first approach, they may not get to spend the money. In fact, it is not uncommon for the provost to periodically *sweep* (take away) departmental fund balance accounts unless the department can argue persuasively that it has a greater need for the money. Why would the provost appear to be so greedy? Obviously, the provost cannot gain personally from sweeping the money. Instead, the provost usually counts on adding this money to the next year's contingency fund to pay for unbudgeted items, ranging from unpredictable start-up or retention requests, novel programmatic initiatives, emergency maintenance and repair expenses, faculty travel to meetings, and so forth. Provosts need money for these kinds of items that ultimately benefit the departments. The alternative to sweeping would be underallocating revenues in the original budgets. So the question for the department chair or the dean boils down to how they want to contribute to the provost's contingency fund, or, more colloquially, "how do you want your medicine?"

Negative fund balances are another story. In most public and many private universities, they must be brought into balance. This involves a budget transfer to equalize expenditures and revenues. There are two approaches to doing so: transferring expenditures to some other account (or accounts) with positive fund balances or transferring revenue from some other account (or accounts) with positive fund balances. In either approach, the budget transfer may be made without any strings attached (which rewards bad management) or, more likely, considered a loan, with a promise to repay the loan from future years' budgets. For example, when the provost offsets a department's negative fund balance by adding the necessary revenue to the department's budget, it is not uncommon for the provost to reduce the department's budget the following year by the amount of the offset unless the department can argue persuasively that the university benefited from the overspending of the budgeted amount. In that case, the budget transfer is considered a subsidy rather than a loan. Of course, budget unit directors must adjust revenues and expenditures in future budgets to avert recurring negative fund balances (and to keep their jobs).

Sponsored Project Post-Award Financial Reports

Sponsored-project budget years do not necessarily coincide with the university's fiscal year. Awards begin and end at various times during the year, depending on the agencies' timetables. As a result, sponsored-projects budgets are closed at various times during the year. The closing procedures resemble those for the university's operating budget, but several reporting and cash management features differ.

Most federal agencies require the university to file an annual report, the Federal Financial Report (FFR), that documents cash receipts, cash disbursements, cash on hand, award amounts, and related financial information for each project.[3] In this context, cash disbursements are the sum of actual cash disbursements for direct charges for goods and services, the amount of indirect expenses charged to the award, and the amount of cash advances and payments made to subcontractors and contractors. These reports are due usually within 90 days after the end of a budget period; budget periods are one year in most cases. Notably, some agencies that require reimbursement (or advance payment) requests on a project-by-project basis (instead of a summary basis), such as the National Science Foundation, do not require these FFRs because their payment management systems extract the same information from the reimbursement and advance payment requests.

If there is an unobligated fund balance at the end of a budget period, the university may ask the funding agency to have it carried over to the next budget period. Or, if there is an unobligated fund balance but no further budget period because the award ended, the university may ask for a one-year no-cost extension of the grant. Carryovers and no-cost extensions do not increase the total amount of the award. They simply extend the time period for spending the award. Agencies usually approve these requests for an additional year.

A final FFR, sometimes known as the Financial Status Report (FSR), must be submitted within 90 days after the end-date of the entire project. This report is the counterpart to the university's financial statement. According to the National Institutes of Health, for example, these final FFRs "must indicate the exact balance of unobligated funds and may not reflect any unliquidated obligations. There must be no discrepancies between the Federal share of expenditures reported on the final FFR and the net cash disbursement [to the university]."[4] Clearly, the amount received by the university (recorded as revenue) must match the expenditures reported to the agency in the FFR. So the grants management office diligently reconciles grant and contract accounts to ensure that authorized amounts, expenditures, and receipts recorded in the university accounting system and the FFR are in agreement.

After the ninety-day period, the accounts are closed. No further drawdowns of federal money are permitted using the agencies' cash management systems, and all unobligated funds must be returned to the funding agency. Fortunately, most agencies allow for adjustments (up or down) in the final FFR for up to fifteen months after the award has closed. In that respect, the federal agencies' closing timeline is much longer than the university's. Thus, if the institution receives a late-arriving, or "trailing," invoice after the ninety-day closure deadline but before the fifteen-month deadline, it may submit a revised FFR requesting reimbursement for the invoiced expenditure. Of course, there must be sufficient unobligated funds to cover this reimbursement; total reimbursements cannot exceed the amount awarded.

As the fiscal year comes to an end, universities launch new budgets, and the cycle begins anew, repeating itself every year into the future. At some point along the way in this never-ending process, time must be taken to reflect on the budget in less quantitative terms: more philosophically, so to speak. Those reflections are the topic of the concluding chapter.

Chapter 8

Power of the Budget

Budgets exert power, the power of money. Conventionally, the power of money derives from what money buys. Within the university, money buys faculty members, higher salaries, research support, scholarships, conference travel, and on and on. In that regard, the amount of money in the budget determines the quality of life on campus: a faculty member's teaching load, a student's financial aid, a dean's ability to launch new initiatives. Accordingly, universities constantly seek more money by lobbying state and federal legislators, developing marketing strategies to attract students, soliciting donations from alumni, and so forth.

The power of the budget constitutes an essential force influencing most aspects of the academic community, both directly and indirectly. Indeed, the budget is the dominant influence in many aspects of the university. This chapter explores several manifestations of this influence.

Insatiable Demand for Money

Budgets play a dominant role in academia because of the university's insatiable demand for money. Axiomatically, every budget unit could accomplish much more if only it had more money in the budget. An anecdote makes this point. A public university president was asked by a state legislator: "How much money does it cost to run the university?" The president answered: "How much do you have?" In other words, "We need every dollar you have." Give the university more money, and it could improve teaching effectiveness by reducing class size, updating computer labs, and providing countless other improvements. The list of possibilities is endless, making the need for more money unappeasable. Even Harvard University, with an endowment of nearly $40 billion, still regularly solicits money from its alumnae donor base by using undergraduates in telemarketing.

Benign examples of this demand for money occur routinely. When a department chair or a dean is asked about the budget, the usual answer is something like "If we had more money, we could improve our services." This is not necessarily a complaint; rather it is a reflexive response, because for most departments, available revenues determine the extent of their service activities. The demand carries over into social interactions. When a faculty member meets a department chair or, going up the hierarchy, a chair meets a dean at a social gathering, the budget often emerges as a topic of conversation, however fleeting.

Two less obvious demands for money warrant more detailed attention: operating reserves and program reviews. In subtle ways, they manifest the institution's pervasive desire for more money.

Operating Reserves

Prudent budget unit directors at all levels in the hierarchy strive to maintain discretionary funds in reserve to buffer financial uncertainties and to provide money for items not in the budget. The contingency funds derived from underallocation of the budget (chapter 6) constitute a prime example. In general, they are available for current-year expenditures and in many universities do not carry forward to the next budget year—at least not at the department and college levels. To maintain fund balances for longer periods of time, allowing them to accumulate, they are transferred into specific *reserve accounts*, indicating that they are not available for current expenditures. Instead, they are set aside for future financial emergencies or unusual opportunities.

At the campus level, the CFO usually administers an important reserve account called the *operating reserve*. An operating reserve is an unrestricted fund balance set aside to stabilize the university's finances by providing a cushion against rainy-day events such as unexpected losses of revenue and large unbudgeted expenditures and to take advantage of serendipitous opportunities. As such, operating reserves are used to cover temporary needs, not structural long-term financial problems. Commonly, they are invested in short-term (one to three years) and long-term (three to seven years) pools, which provide for liquidity and growth, respectively. In some institutions, they are managed as part of the endowment.

Operating reserves are an important aspect of university finances. Indeed, governing boards commonly require them. Accordingly, they constitute a major responsibility for the CFO. In a survey of CFOs of nonprofit organizations, the Center on Philanthropy found that nearly 40 percent of respondents identified maintenance of operating cash reserves and financial flexibility as their organization's primary financial objective for the upcoming fiscal year.[1]

How much cash is needed in the operating reserve? The target amount varies according to institutional exposure to financial risks such as unstable enrollment trends or natural disasters. The rule of thumb is to have sufficient funds to meet at least one payroll cycle or, more commonly, two to six months of operating expenses. In practice, for a conservative CFO, more is better. As the accounting firm Grant Thornton observes, "Based on our experience with finance professionals across the nonprofit sector, few executives consider their organization to be 'well-funded'; in fact, most believe that their reserves are significantly underfunded."[2] In these cases, the demand for money may not be insatiable, but it is considerable.

Functionally, positive fund balances in the operating budget constitute a major source of money for operating reserve accounts. In fact, the CFO may underallocate revenues in the master budget to create a positive fund balance that can be transferred into an operating reserve account. Incidentally, the planned fund balance at the beginning of the fiscal year is sometimes called the *margin*. There are no guidelines concerning the amount that can be underallocated, and the process is generally "invisible" to most faculty members. Greater transparency is achieved when budget transfers into reserve accounts are itemized in the budget.

Some governing boards impose restrictions on the amount and the source of money held in the operating reserve. For example, the University of Hawaii Board of Regents calls for the university to maintain operating reserves "sufficient to provide for continued operations of the university for a minimum of two months."[3] Significantly, however, the operating reserves must be derived from non–general fund revenues. Other universities impose similar guidelines.

Budget units lower in the hierarchy may also establish operating reserve accounts. It is common practice in auxiliary units and in universities using revenue-based budget models, such as RCM. There are many good reasons for a provost, dean, department chair, or principal investigator of a large grant to build up a sizable reserve account—amounting to more than about $100,000. Of course, a primary rationale is financial stability. In addition, for a provost, dean, or department chair at a research university, a common rationale is future start-up packages for new faculty members, which can be very costly (sometimes more than $1 million). Principal investigators also may hold grant money in reserve to cover a reduced grant budget, unexpected expenditures owing to technical challenges, and other emergencies. In general, the existence of these reserves explains why a provost, dean, or department chair can appear to have a stash of discretionary money. In fact, they do.

Operating reserves can be a contentious issue on campus. Indeed, taking money out of the institution's everyday operations to build up reserves can provoke rumors and suspicions of hoarding by greedy administrators. For example, a vacant faculty position may go unfilled or routine building maintenance may be curtailed as a way of building up the reserves. Questions arise: Why does the vice president for finance need all that money in reserve when our department is so broke? The administration (provost, CFO, and president) should have a credible answer to that question.

In times of budgetary stress, these reserves look very attractive to cash-hungry CFOs, legislative budget personnel, and governing board members. Unspent funds can be swept—taken away—to cover other university needs. These administrators (the "sweepers") may acknowledge that a sweep punishes what might seem to be solid conservative management by the reserve account holders. Nonetheless, in tight times, there may be few other alternative sources of cash to meet budgetary shortfalls. As pointed out in *Managing the Research University*, "experienced chief research officers routinely keep an eye on these unspent research-related balances and issue warnings about potential sweeps. One common ploy against 'the sweep' is to distribute unspent money into many smaller reserve accounts to reduce their visibility on the chief financial officer's radar screen."[4] As a best practice, a less cunning strategy is to have clear, well-communicated policies about the purpose, amounts, and sources of reserve funds.

Program Reviews

The quest for more money seeps into the academic infrastructure. In some cases, this quest can erode institutional governance. A prime example occurs during *program reviews*, periodic reviews of campus academic departments, centers, institutes, and so forth. Many reviewers succumb to the temptation of suggesting that the program needs additional institutional support to thrive or to achieve greatness. They might say: "If it just had another million dollars, the center could step up to the next level." With good intentions, they seek to leverage more support from the budget using the promise of better programmatic performance as a lever. With less noble intentions, they imply that the budget constrains the program from achieving greatness. Used that way, the budget is a sinister impediment.

Unfortunately, this kind of commentary is not helpful to the provost. Axiomatically, any academic unit, including the university as a whole, can benefit from more money. As in most educational endeavors, more money buys additional resources and, by inference, enhanced quality. Therefore, to predicate an academic review on additional funding compromises the review's value, for it puts the provost in a difficult position: If the provost is not prepared to provide the recommended funding, then why bother reading the review at all? Thus, as a best practice, review committee members should be instructed a priori to concentrate on the performance achieved or achievable solely with the available resources. Take the budget out of the review process. The performance review is not the place to ask for more money.

This important point can be debated further. The debate begins with the assertion that a review committee is expected to recommend areas of improvement and promising directions to follow. A question arises: Isn't it implicit that money will be needed to follow these recommendations? The answer is: maybe. But the academic program must figure out how to accomplish its goals within its budgetary constraints. The program should not be forced into a situation where it cannot meet the review's recommendations without additional funding, especially if there is little chance that it can get the money. A second question arises: If budgets are tight, as they always seem to be, is the review process a waste of effort? The answer is: no. Stripping away these budgetary concerns, a review nearly always helps. At the very least it requires a self-study, which, if thoughtfully prepared, can be of great value to the program. By the way, if the self-study is not thoughtfully prepared, the program director should be reprimanded and probably replaced.

Change

Budgets have the power to change universities. That power relates directly to the power of money. It is exerted in every budget cycle, when expenditure authorization is allocated to the budget units. Changes in the budget's revenue allocations mean that the budget units must adjust their operations according to their new allocations. In this, they follow the money. In fact, the budget units have little say in the matter; if their budget changes, they must change accordingly.

Slow Incremental Changes

Change does not come easily for universities. Indeed it usually occurs at a very slow pace, with relatively small incremental changes in the budget every year. The reasons for the slow pace of change emanate from the university's self-image. Traditionally, universities view themselves as lasting forever. For that reason, they tend to make long commitments. As Frederick Balderston points out in *Managing Today's University*, "The expectation of permanence imparts more deliberateness to the university's attitude toward change than is true of many other organizations, for which the rule is: change or die."[5] Despite their presumption of permanence, universities plan their budgets one year at a time. Even so, the incremental budget model conveys a sense of institutional longevity, with little incentive for change.

At their inherently slow pace, universities evolve as resources are reallocated in the budget. Ideally, these gradual reallocations conform to the evolving strategic plan. In that sense, the slow pace is an advantage. For example, while preparing the operating budget, the provost may decide to increase a high-priority department's authorized expenditures, perhaps by enough to hire a new faculty or staff member. This increase may come at the expense of some other lower-priority department, whose authorized expenditures are decreased (for example, a vacancy is recaptured), or result from an investment of windfall revenue. Incremental decisions like this do not bring about major changes by themselves, but over time they alter the university's character. For a medium-sized department (about 15 faculty members), the addition of 3 new faculty members over a five-year period can make a significant difference.

Transformative Changes

Occasionally, evolutionary pressures force transformative changes in the university's budget, and therefore the university. These pressures may come from external sources beyond the university's control, including reduced revenues associated with unexpected shifts in local demographics, student academic interests, federal research funding priorities, the local economy, or societal needs. Pressures may also arise when the university receives a large donation, such as money for a new building or school. Less commonly, transformative budget changes result from internal events: a budget unit loses accreditation; a large, sustaining grant is not renewed; a group of highly productive faculty members move to another university. In all of these examples, necessary budget adjustments serve as a strong push that overcomes inertia. Without this push, the inertia that prevents significant changes to the budget is difficult—though not impossible—to overcome, even during periods of financial stress.

Transformative changes evoke major adjustments in resource allocations within the budget. In the jargon, the budget is *rebalanced*. If significant new revenue (for example, a large donation) becomes available, the rebalancing is additive; money is added to one or more budget units. In these fortunate situations, rebalancing the budget is relatively easy. Budget units do not complain, because they do not lose money. In contrast, if significant new revenue is not available, money must be reallocated from one budget unit to another. Budget units will complain if they perceive that their budget is losing resources to new initiatives in some other budget unit. Understandably, reallocations are never easy. As a best practice in these situations, multiple constituencies should participate in the decision-making process about who gets what, just as they participate in the strategic planning process.

A formal reallocation plan should accompany a rebalancing of the budget. Otherwise, the process can cause confusion, anxiety, and programmatic damage. For example, because personnel costs consume such a large fraction of most academic budgets, some departments may have to reduce the number of instructors (including faculty members) to accommodate reallocations exceeding about 4 percent of their authorized expenditures. That can be a slow process with further consequences for the overall academic curriculum. As a best practice in this case, a more orderly strategy would be to spread large reallocations over more than one year. Moreover, the impact of the reallocations on other units should be assessed beforehand.

Return on Investment

When rebalancing the budget, universities expect to gain from the reallocations. Otherwise, there is no reason to disrupt status quo. The expectation usually involves money somehow, either directly or indirectly. Stated more bluntly, universities invest money in academic programs, faculty members, or facilities with the expectation of monetary return. The financial *return on investment* (ROI) may come from many potential sources, including tuition income generated by increased student enrollment, more efficient teaching assignments, and more grant awards, royalties, and licensing income.

A hypothetical example occurs when student enrollment increases in computer science courses but decreases in history courses. To accommodate this shift in demand and the corresponding need for instructors, the dean of arts and sciences recaptures two faculty positions in history and reallocates them to computer sciences. When making this reallocation, the dean most probably considers the ROI: two new faculty members can attract more students and generate more tuition revenue in computer science than in history. Prompted by the potential ROI, the dean has brought about change.

Another hypothetical example occurs when a newly hired faculty member in engineering is given start-up funds to establish an independent research program. Implicitly, the faculty member is expected to generate income for the university from grant funds within several years. For the university, reimbursed indirect costs yield the best ROI, mainly because they are unrestricted, unlike direct costs. Therefore, the faculty member is specifically expected to generate indirect cost reimbursement from federal grants within several years. This expectation may not be written explicitly in an employment contract, but it is usually made quite clear by the dean or department chair.

Politically, the ROI concept illustrated by these two examples is unpalatable to many faculty members. It places a mercenary pall on the academic profession. Nevertheless, among deans and higher-level administrators, ROI is widely accepted as a financial metric in the budgetary decision-making process.

In quantitative terms, the relationship between the investment and the return, the ROI, is expressed as a percentage:

$$\text{ROI} = \frac{(\text{Return} - \text{Investment})}{\text{Investment}} \times 100\%.$$

So if the computer science department receives $500,000 in funds reallocated from the history department for five years of a new faculty member's salary (the investment), and within five years the new faculty member generates $1.5 million in additional tuition revenue (the return), then

$$\text{ROI} = \frac{(1,500,000 - 500,000)}{500,000} \times 100\% = 200\%.$$

In this case, the university doubled its money in five years. Through reallocation, it invested $500,000 in computer science and earned a net $1,000,000 (that is, $1,500,000 minus $500,000). This is a very good positive return. (Before drawing conclusions, however, it is important to evaluate how reallocating this $500,000 affects the income generated by the history department. What if it now generates $1.5 million less in tuition revenue?)

Understandably, the ROI may not always be positive. In this example, if the additional tuition generated by the computer science department is less than the $500,000 investment, the ROI would be negative. The university would not have lost money, but the reallocation would not necessarily have been a good investment. Naturally, that is not desirable. If the department generates $500,000, the return equals the investment, and the ROI would be zero and the university would break even. Few universities expect an ROI less than 0 percent. At the very least, they expect to break even.

Indeed, a positive ROI is the goal of most strategic investments in individual faculty members. In a nonresearch environment, a newly hired faculty member may be expected to teach several undergraduate courses each year. The salary constitutes the investment, and tuition income constitutes the return. In a research environment, a newly hired faculty member may be expected to generate grant funds yielding an ROI of at least 200 percent. The salary and start-up costs constitute the investment, and the indirect cost reimbursement constitutes the return. If the target ROI is not met because of insufficient enrollment in one or more courses or insufficient grant funds, the faculty member may be assigned additional responsibilities. A football coach is expected to win games. The coaching-staff salaries, player scholarships, equipment, and stadium facilities constitute the investment, and ticket sales, broadcast revenue, and donations constitute the return. If the ROI is not met, the coach is fired. And so it goes for investments throughout the campus.

Legal Aspects of the Budget

Through a philosophical lens, budgets are organic. In this context, "organic" does not refer to carbon atoms or pesticide-free. Rather, it refers to a more arcane concept: "of, relating to, or constituting the law by which a government or organization exists"[6] Parsing that definition, "organic" relates to a law, defined as "a binding custom or practice of a community: a rule of conduct or action prescribed or formally recognized as binding or enforced by a controlling authority."[7] The budget is thus organic because it serves as a binding force that guides the university's actions. By inference, all activities must conform to any constraints imposed by the budget.

Is a university budget really a law or a contract that can be enforced in the courts? As usual in legal matters, the answer is, it depends. Therefore, the question will be rephrased in the context of several specific circumstances.

The Budget as a Law

At the federal and state level, the appropriations budget is de facto law. It authorizes the university to spend the appropriated resources for agreed-upon services, such as teaching, research, and public service. However, the university must abide by any budgetary constraints imposed by the Congress or legislature in the appropriations process. The State of California asserts this explicitly: "Departments have the primary responsibility to operate within budgeted levels and to comply with any restrictions or limitations enacted by the Legislature. Further, the general expectation is that State agencies comply with the legislative intent."[8] The language of the appropriations acts does not always clearly express legislative intent, so debate transcripts, early drafts, and committee notes related to the appropriations bills are generally reviewed to ascertain what the legislature had in mind when it crafted the appropriations. Failure to conform to the enacted budget and to honor legislative intent could have legal repercussions for university administrators and jeopardize future legislative appropriations. It is comparable to biting the hand that feeds you.

Technically, these legal constraints prevent the university from spending more than the appropriated funds for specified services, regardless of changes in the services delivered. As stated in federal and state constitutions, "No Money shall be drawn from the Treasury, but in Consequence of Appropriations made by Law."[9] Thus, if enrollment increases significantly after completion of the appropriation process, the university cannot spend more public money than has been appropriated to meet increased demand. It must deliver more services at a lower cost per student, seek a supplemental appropriation, or use revenue from some private source. In this way, the legislature retains control directly over university spending and indirectly over services provided by the university. This pertains to all public universities and any private universities receiving government funding.

Fortunately, states allow flexibility in this regard. Although the university cannot spend more than the appropriated amount, generally it may adjust its budget to accommodate changing needs. Such an adjustment may require approval by the governor's office and possibly the legislature. In California, for example, "the Legislature has also provided provisions in the Budget Act to allow for budget adjustments. Most of this authority requires Director of Finance approval; many require a formal notice to the Legislature and a waiting period to provide the opportunity for legislative review and response before final approval."[10] Some states provide lump-sum appropriations, free of any legislative constraints. In those cases, the governing board and, by delegation, the president and CFO have the authority to change the spending plan whenever financial conditions change unexpectedly.

The Budget as a Contract

Within the university, budgets are not considered contracts. That is important, because contracts are enforceable in the courts, which hold both parties accountable for fulfilling the terms of the contract and levy consequences for failing to do so. Because of this importance, the rationale for asserting that budgets are not contracts merits clarification.

Fundamentally, there are four essential elements of a legally binding contract according to common law:

- offer
- acceptance
- consideration
- intention to create a legal relationship

Does the budget process encompass these four elements? From a distance, it might appear so. In the university budgeting process, the governing board, through the CFO, offers the budget units in the hierarchy the authority to commit university resources according to the budget. In return for its offer, the governing board receives consideration: teaching, research, and service. There is some give and take in the budgeting process, but the budget units routinely accept this offer. Looking at this more closely, a cynic might ask: "What other choice do the budget units have? They work for the governing board; teaching, research, and service are conditions of employment. So refusing the offer constitutes insubordination." From this perspective, the budget process does not rise to the level of formal offers and acceptances inherent in contracts, nor does it conform to the contractual concept of consideration. Apropos of the fourth element, both the governing board and the budget units enter into the budgeting process in good faith, tantamount to creating a legal relationship. But in reality the governing board's fiduciary responsibilities take precedence over the budgetary relationships. All in all, budgets do not encompass the four essential elements of a contract and, therefore, do not have the force of law.

Although budgets are not legally enforceable contracts, they do represent an understanding between parties with implicit commitments about acceptable forms of behavior. In this context, what remedy do budget units have if projected revenues do not materialize and the CFO cannot provide the full amount authorized in the original budget? None, really. At best, the budget unit may be allowed to commensurately reduce the level of expected services. Conversely, what remedy does the provost have if a budget unit does not perform all of the services implied in the budget owing to low student interest, for example? Once more, the answer is none, at least until the next year's budget, when compensatory adjustments can be made. Another question follows: Can the university bring suit against a budget director who overspends? In the absence of a specific contractual performance agreement or criminal activity, the answer is no. Budget directors are employees of the university. Therefore, if their overspending is linked to their failure to satisfactorily carry out the duties and responsibilities of their positions, then the university could take appropriate employment remedies, including termination.

These questions can be extended to the level of individual faculty members: Can a faculty member bring suit against the university if it denies some expenditure authorized in the budget? There are so many variables in this scenario that it is difficult to give a universal answer. For starters, assume that the denied expenditure is something specific and concrete, such as a travel reimbursement or, more starkly, a due salary payment. The aggrieved faculty member could go to court and state a claim against the university. Several legal theories would be available to the faculty member, such as breach of contract or unjust enrichment. Conceivably, there might be a valid case against the university. Alternatively, assume that the denied expenditure is something less concrete, such as: "My department was promised funding to hire a new lecturer to help teach my course, but we never got the position number." In this simple case, the disgruntled faculty member most probably would not prevail in court. Of course, more complicated factual scenarios can be imagined that might give rise to some sort of legal claim. For example, suppose the faculty member was induced to turn down a lucrative offer of employment at another university by a promise that the next year's budget would contain additional money for a lecturer to help teach the faculty member's course. If the promised money was not delivered, the faculty member may have a legal claim for promissory estoppel or even fraud. But the promise must have been in writing and signed by the appropriate university official.

The bottom line is this: unlike a formal contract, a budget represents a statement of the university's programmatic priorities and a means of financing ongoing operations. Although there are advantages to viewing the budget as a contract, in reality, it cannot be seen as more than an implicit commitment that cannot be enforced in the courts except in very specific situations. Incidentally, even if a lawsuit against a public university were successful, sovereign immunity would likely limit the extent of any monetary remedy.

The law and contracts aside, in practice, budgets confer assurances, at least to personnel with indefinite appointments. If their names appear in the budget, those individuals (for example, faculty members) may assume that their employment is secure. An anecdote illustrates this point. After several months on the job, a newly appointed faculty member told the department chair: "I never received a contract. Where is it?" In reply, the veteran chair said: "Why do you need a contract? You're in the budget." In that case, the budget presumably constitutes evidence of agreed-upon terms of employment, specifying fundamental aspects of the appointment, such as the job title, percent effort, salary, and fringe benefit costs. But it does not specify other terms of employment, such as workload expectations, vacation, sick leave, and termination clauses. At best, those other terms are described in a faculty handbook, which, incidentally, most universities declare is not a contract.

This study of university budgets began metaphorically in the opening sentence of the preface: as planets revolve around the sun, universities revolve around the budget. Now, in conclusion, the opening metaphor can be modified to make a less celestial point: as money makes the world go around, the budget makes the university go around. Through the philosophical lens, that has been the point all along.

Notes

Chapter 1. The Language of Budgets

1. AccountingTools, "Asset definition," accessed February 21, 2019, http://www.accountingtools.com/definition-asset.

2. AccountingTools, "Liability," accessed February 21, 2019, http://www.accountingtools.com/definition-liability.

3. Financial Accounting Standards Board, "Not-for-Profit Entities Presentation of Financial Statements Glossary," accessed February 21, 2019, https://asc.fasb.org/glossary&letter=N.

4. Financial Accounting Standards Board, "Not-for-Profit Entities Presentation of Financial Statements Glossary," accessed February 21, 2019, https://asc.fasb.org/glossary&letter=F.

5. National Association of College and University Business Officers, "Reporting Expenses," accessed February 21, 2019, http://efarm.nacubo.org/farm/s010.

6. *Oxford Dictionaries*, s.v. "account," accessed February 21, 2019, https://en.oxforddictionaries.com/?utm_source=od-panel&utm_campaign=en.

7. *Cambridge Dictionary*, s.v. "budgetary accounting," accessed July 6, 2017, http://dictionary.cambridge.org/us/dictionary/english/budgetary-accounting.

8. *Oxford Dictionaries*, s.v. "fund," accessed March 5, 2019, https://en.oxforddictionaries.com/definition/fund.

9. Governmental Accounting Standards Board, "Fund Balance: It May Not Be What You Think It Is," May 2006, accessed December 28, 2016, http://www.gasb.org/cs/ContentServer?pagename=GASB%2FGASBContent_C%2FUsersArticlePage&cid=1176156737123.

10. BusinessDictionary, s.v. "encumbrance," accessed March 17, 2016, http://www.businessdictionary.com/definition/encumbrance.html.

Chapter 2. University Budgets

1. *Oxford Dictionaries*, s.v. "budget," accessed November 23, 2015, https://en.oxforddictionaries.com/definition/budget.
2. BusinessDictionary, s.v. "budget," accessed March 17, 2016, http://www.businessdictionary.com/definition/budget.html.
3. Oxford Dictionaries, s.v. "budget."
4. Internal Revenue Service, *Tax-Exempt Governmental Bonds*, Publication 4079 (Washington, DC: IRS, 2016).
5. Dean O. Smith, *University Finances: Accounting and Budgeting Principles for Higher Education* (Baltimore: Johns Hopkins University Press, 2019), p. 382.
6. Office of Management and Budget, "Uniform Administrative Requirements, Cost Principles, and Audit Requirements for Federal Awards, 2 C.F.R. § 200," accessed June 19, 2017, http://www.ecfr.gov/cgi-bin/text-idx?tpl=/ecfrbrowse/Title02/2cfr200_main_02.tpl.
7. Michelle A. Aloia, "Position Control as a Best Practice," accessed July 5, 2018, cacubo.org/wp-content/uploads/2016/05/PositionControl.pdf.

Chapter 3. Budget Models

1. *Oxford Dictionaries*, s.v. "model," accessed November 23, 2015, https://en.oxforddictionaries.com/definition/model.
2. Texas Higher Education Coordinating Board, "The Budgeting Process for Public Universities in Texas," accessed February 23, 2019, http://www.thecb.state.tx.us/reports/PDF/10218.PDF?CFID=73742955&CFTOKEN=23838753.
3. Texas Higher Education Coordinating Board, "Budgeting Process."
4. University of Washington, "Activity Based Budgeting," accessed July 3, 2016, http://opb.washington.edu/activity-based-budgeting.
5. AccountingTools, "The Responsibility Center," accessed February 23, 2019, http://www.accountingtools.com/questions-and-answers/what-is-a-responsibility-center.html.
6. John R. Curry, Andrew L. Laws, and Jon C. Strauss, *Responsibility Center Management: A Guide to Balancing Academic Entrepreneurship with Fiscal Responsibility*, 2nd ed. (Washington, DC: National Association of College and University Business Officers, 2013).

7. Bethany Nolan, "How It Works: A Basic Guide to IU's Budget Model," accessed February 23, 2019, http://archive.inside.indiana.edu/editors-picks/campus-life/2016-06-01-university-budget-model.shtml; University of Michigan, "About the U-M Budget Model," accessed July 18, 2016, http://obp.umich.edu/root/budget/budget-about/; University of Pennsylvania, "Responsibility Center Management," accessed February 23, 2019, http://www.budget.upenn.edu/dlDocs/rcm.pdf.

8. Mallory Barnes and Kyle Clark, "Responsibility Center Management: The Good, the Bad, and the Ugly," accessed February 23, 2019, https://www.nacubo.org/-/media/Nacubo/Documents/EventsandPrograms/2013PBF/Responsibility-Center-Management-Presentation.ashx; Leroy W. Dubeck, "Beware Higher Ed's Newest Budget Twist," *Thought and Action (The NEA Higher Education Journal)*, Spring 2007, pp. 81–91, accessed March 19, 2018, http://www.nea.org/assets/img/PubThoughtAndAction/TAA_97Spr_07.pdf.

9. Dubeck, "Beware Higher Ed's Newest Budget Twist."

10. Curry, Laws, and Strauss, *Responsibility Center Management*, pp. 23, 79–80.

Chapter 4. Strategic Plans

1. Portions of this chapter are extracted from pp. 40–46 in Dean O. Smith, *Managing the Research University* (New York: Oxford University Press, 2011). By permission of Oxford University Press, http://www.oup.com.

2. Western Association of Schools and Colleges Senior College and University Commission, "Standard 4: Creating an Organization Committed to Quality Assurance, Institutional Learning, and Improvement § 4.6," *2013 Handbook of Accreditation,* rev. ed. (2018), accessed June 15, 2018, https://www.wscuc.org/book/export/html/924.

3. Steven A. Finkler et al., *Financial Management for Public, Health, and Not-for-Profit Organizations*, 5th ed. (Thousand Oaks, CA: CQ Press, 2017), p. 25.

4. University of North Carolina at Chapel Hill, "About the Graduate School: The Graduate School's Mission," accessed September 5, 2018, https://gradschool.unc.edu/about/aboutus.html.

5. Cornell University, "A Strategic Plan 2010–2015," accessed June 18, 2018, https://cornell-classic.univcomm.cornell.edu/strategicplan/commitments.cfm.

Chapter 5. Operating Budget Preparation

1. Adapted from Dean O. Smith, *University Finances: Accounting and Budgeting Principles for Higher Education* (Baltimore: Johns Hopkins University Press, 2019), p. 177.

2. Lucie Lapovsky and Loren Loomis Hubbell, "Financial Aid: Does It Matter Whether It's Funded? No," *Business Officer* 39, no. 1 (2005), p. 48.

3. Uniform Law Commission, "Prudent Management of Institutional Funds Act," accessed February 24, 2019, https://www.uniformlaws.org/viewdocument/final-act-no-comments-58?CommunityKey=043b9067-bc2c-46b7-8436-07c9054064a3&tab=librarydocuments, § 4(d).

4. Smith, *University Finances,* pp. 179–80.

5. James Frew, Robert Olson, and M. Lee Pelton, "Creating a Flexible Budget Process: Contingency Budgeting Is One Response to Economic Uncertainty," *Academe* (November–December 2009), accessed August 10, 2018, https://www.aaup.org/article/creating-flexible-budget-process#.W23j5rhMFPY.

6. Smith, *University Finances*, p. 99.

7. Commonfund Institute, "Higher Education Price Index," accessed March 25, 2018, https://www.commonfund.org/commonfund-institute/higher-education-price-index-hepi/; Department of Labor, Bureau of Labor Statistics, "Consumer Price Index," accessed April 16, 2018, https://www.bls.gov/cpi/.

8. James Surowiecki, *The Wisdom of Crowds: Why the Many Are Smarter Than the Few and How Collective Wisdom Shapes Business, Economies, Societies and Nations* (New York: Doubleday, 2004).

9. Southern Association of Colleges and Schools Commission on Colleges, "Principles of Accreditation: Foundation for Quality Enhancement" (2012), accessed May 4, 2016, http://www.sacscoc.org/principles.asp, § 2.11.1.

10. Margaret J. Barr and George S. McClellan, *Budgets and Financial Management in Higher Education*, 2nd ed. (San Francisco: Jossey-Bass, 2011); Larry Goldstein, *A Guide to College and University Budgeting: Foundations for Institutional Effectiveness*, 4th ed. (Washington, DC: National Association of College and Business Officers, 2012).

11. Elizabeth Hamilton Foley, "The Budgeting Process," Nonprofit Accounting Basics: Reporting and Operations (2010), accessed

August 10, 2018, https://www.nonprofitaccountingbasics.org
/reporting-operations/budgeting-process.

Chapter 6. Budget Implementation

1. Stanford University, "Administrative Guide, University Funds, 5. Budgeting," accessed April 13, 2016, https://adminguide.stanford.edu /chapter-3/subchapter-1/policy-3-1-2.
2. Stanford University, "Budget Management: Variance Reporting: Variance Reporting Process Guide," accessed March 7, 2018, https://web.stanford.edu/group/fms/fingate/docs/budget/howto /Tidemark_BBudget_YearEnd_VarRept.pdf.
3. Lucie Lapovsky and Loren Loomis Hubbell, "Financial Aid: Does It Matter Whether It's Funded? No," *Business Officer* 39, no. 1 (2005), p. 51.
4. Lapovsky and Hubbell, "Financial Aid," p. 51.
5. Dean O. Smith, *Understanding Authority in Higher Education* (Lanham, MD: Rowman and Littlefield, 2015), p. 45.
6. Dean O. Smith, *University Finances: Accounting and Budgeting Principles for Higher Education* (Baltimore: Johns Hopkins University Press, 2019), p. 203.

Chapter 7. End of the Fiscal Year

1. Larry Goldstein, *A Guide to College and University Budgeting: Foundations for Institutional Effectiveness*, 4th ed. (Washington, DC: National Association of College and University Business Officers, 2012), p. 202.
2. Dean O. Smith, *University Finances: Accounting and Budgeting Principles for Higher Education* (Baltimore, MD: Johns Hopkins University Press, 2019), pp. 215–239.
3. National Institutes of Health, "Federal Financial Report (FFR)," accessed February 26, 2019, https://grants.nih.gov/grants/forms /report_on_grant/federal_financial_report_ffr.htm.
4. National Institutes of Health, *NIH Grants Policy Statement* (Bethesda, MD: NIH, 2018), § 8.6.1, accessed February 26, 2019, https://grants .nih.gov/grants/policy/nihgps/nihgps.pdf.

Chapter 8. Power of the Budget

1. Center on Philanthropy at Indiana University, *Financial Literacy and Knowledge in the Nonprofit Sector* (Bloomington: Indiana University,

2012), accessed February 27, 2019, www.philanthropy.iupui.edu/files
/research/2012financialliteracy.pdf.

2. Grant Thornton LLP, *Reserves Planning: A Step-by-Step Approach for Nonprofit Organizations* (Chicago: Grant Thornton, 2013), accessed February 27, 2019, https://www.grantthornton.com/~/media/content -page-files/nfp/pdfs/2013/130516-NFP-Reserves-Planning-White-Paper -130916.ashx.

3. University of Hawaii, "Operating Reserves; Non-General Funds," Board of Regents Policy 8.203, accessed December 28, 2016, http:// hawaii.edu/policy/?action=viewPolicy&policySection =rp&policyChapter=8&policyNumber=203&menuView=open.

4. Dean O. Smith, *Managing the Research University* (New York: Oxford University Press, 2011), p. 58.

5. Frederick E. Balderston, *Managing Today's University*, 2nd ed. (San Francisco: Jossey-Bass, 1995), p. 91.

6. Merriam-Webster, s.v. "organic," accessed August 22, 2018, https:// www.merriam-webster.com/dictionary/organic.

7. Merriam-Webster, s.v. "law," accessed February 20, 2019, https:// www.merriam-webster.com/dictionary/law.

8. State of California, "California's Budget Process," accessed March 1, 2019, http://www.dof.ca.gov/budget/Budget_Process/index.html.

9. U.S. Const., art. I, § 9.7.

10. State of California, "California's Budget Process."

Index

accounting: accrual basis of, 142, 144-45; budgetary, 11, 16, 69; cash basis of, 11-12, 142, 144-45; double-entry, 7-10, 142; encumbrance, 16-17; financial, 11; fund, 12, 14-15, 20; fundamental equation of, 3, 14, 142; terminology, 2, 17

accounts: chart of, 13-14; definition of, 6; reserve, 113; subaccounts, 6; types of, 6-7

accreditation associations, 74, 78, 84, 108

alignment, budget and strategic plan, 73, 83-84

apportionment, 112-13

appropriations, state: as capital budget revenue, 31, 34; in the consolidated budget, 29-31; every tub on its own bottom, 69; formula-based allocation of, 55-56; as law, 164-66; legislative intent, 165; as operating budget revenue, 21-22; projections of, 95, 101, 104; restrictions on, 21-22; revised budgets, 123, 126; structural deficits, 131-32; and subvention, 58, 65

assets: capital, 31-35, 113; in the chart of accounts, 14; definition of, 3; double-entry accounting,

7-8; in the financial statements, 142-45; in the fundamental accounting equation, 3-4; fund balances, 14-15; and revenues, 4

audit, 9, 140

authority: delegated, 111-12; expiration at fiscal year's end, 136; hiring, 115; human resource data, 25; journal entries, 9; release of funds, 111-12; responsibility center management, 62; revenue allocation, 105; transfers of, 20. *See also* authority to commit university money

authority to commit university money: the budget, 20; budget transfers, 129; expiration at year's end, 136; grant awards, 41; legal aspects of, 164-66

auxiliary enterprises, 37-40, 71

bonds, 32-33, 144

budget: closing of, 137-40, 150-52; cycle, 90-109, 124-26, 152, 159; deficits, 131-32; definition of, 18-21; flexibility of, 126-28; hearings, 49-52, 95, 105-7; hierarchy of, 22-24; implementation of, 83-87, 110-11; the power of, 153; preliminary budget (*cont.*)

planning, 102-7; rebalanced, 124, 160; revised, 123-26; rolling forward, 52, 147; structural surpluses and deficits, 131-35; uncertainties, 45-46, 154; unit, definition of, 22. *See also* budget types

budget, legal aspects of: as a contract, 166-69; as a law, 164-66

budget adjustments: consolidations and closures, 133-35; downsizing, 133; in flexible budgets, 71; in formula-based budget models, 56; recapture, 114-16; rescission, 124-26; retrenchment, 132-33; revision, 123-24; transfers, 128-30, 149-50; and variance mitigation, 126-30

budget consolidation: definition of, 29; in the final budget assembly, 107-8; in the preliminary operating budget process, 91, 103-4; in revised budgets, 127

budget models: activity-based, 57; every tub on its own bottom, 69; formula-based, 52-57; incremental, 49-52, 55, 65; responsibility center management, 62-68; revenue-based, 57-62; static versus flexible, 69-72; zero-based, 48-49

budget process: auxiliary, 90; capital, 34-35, 89; and legal contracts, 166-67; operating, 90-109; revised operating, 124-26

budget transfers: budget adjustments, 128-30; closing the books, 140; in fund accounting, 15; negative fund balances,

149-50; from one fund to another, 39-40; positive fund balances, 156; to reserve accounts, 113

budget types: auxiliary, 37-39, 89-90; base, 24; capital, 31-37, 89, 102; college, 23, 28, 50, 137; consolidated, 23, 29-31; department, 23-28, 50-52; fixed, 69-71; flexible, 69-71; general fund, 22; grant and contract, 41; line-item, 20-21, 25, 28-29; master, 22-23, 29; multi-campus system, 107; operating, 21-24; position, 25, 42-45; project-specific, 41-42; provost's, 22-23, 28-29; static, 69-71, 99-100, 126-28. *See also* operating budget

budget unit, definition of, 22

certificates of participation, 33

change: slow incremental, 159-60; transformative, 160-61

chart of accounts, 13-14

chief budget officer, 17, 111

chief financial officer: authority of, 9, 166; budget cycle decisions, 92; budget revision, 123-26; the capital budget, 33-34; and the chief budget officer, 17, 23; closing the books, 140; the consolidated budget, 108; endowment payout, 96; expenditure projections, 100-102; final revenue projections, 104; and fiscal officers, 9; flexible revenue projections, 99-100, 102; the general ledger, 10; indirect cost reimbursement, 97-98; investment revenue, 97; the operating reserve, 155-57; position control, 43; preliminary revenue projections, 92-100;

release of funds, 111-14; state appropriations, 49, 95-96
closing the books, 140
closing the budget, 137-40, 150-52
consolidations and closures, 133-35
contingency fund: vs. reserve accounts, 154; and sweeping fund balances, 149; underallocation, 113-14
contracts, budgetary accounting of. See grants and contracts
control of revenues and expenditures, 116-22
credits, 7-11, 128-30

debits, 7-11, 128-30
debt financing, 31, 35
deferred maintenance: budget adjustments, 127; budget transfers to, 30, 39, 124; in capital budgets, 37; definition of, 37; and downsizing, 133

edits, software, 24
encumbrance: definition of, 16; liquidation of, 16, 136-39
endowment: income, 21, 57, 95; payout rate, 95-96
expenditures: classification of, 5, 20-21, 25, 39; definition of, 4; inflation adjustments of, 101-2; projections of, 100-102

Federal Financial Report, 150-52
Financial Accounting Standards Board (FASB), 5
financial exigency, 134
financial statements: balance sheet, 142-43; and the budget, 142-44, 146; footnotes, 141; income statement, 143-44;

purpose of, 140-42; statement of cash flows, 144-46
Financial Status Report, 151-52
fiscal officers: and budget transfers, 129; chart of accounts, 13; encumbrance accounting, 16-17; journal entries, 9; purchase order review, 138; spending authority of, 20; transaction review, 117
fiscal year: closing of, 136-40; definition of, 2
flexible revenue projections, 100, 102, 104
fund accounting, 12, 14-15, 20
fundamental accounting equation, 3, 14-15, 142
fund balance: beginning, 14-15; changes in, 143; definition of, 14; and discretionary money, 15; federal grants, 155-56; reserved vs. unreserved, 15; roll forward, 147-49; sweep of, 147; year-end, 147-51
funds: apportionment of, 112; contingency, 113-14; definitions of, 12-13; recapture of, 114-16; release of, 111-14; reserve, 39, 102, 113; transfers between, 15, 39; underallocation of, 113-14

general fund: budget cuts, 132-33; the capital budget, 31, 36; definition of, 22; fund balances, 149; operating reserves, 156
general fund budget, 22. See also operating budget
general ledger, 10
Generally Accepted Accounting Principles (GAAP), 11

Government Accounting Standards Board (GASB), 141
grants and contracts: accounts, 6; budget closing, 151-52; budget projections, 97-98, 104; carryover of, 151; in the consolidated budget, 29; fund accounting, 12; no-cost extension of, 151; in the operating budget, 21-22; program closures, 135; project-specific budgets, 41; reserved funds, 15; return on investment, 161-64; revenue-based budgeting, 59-62; statement of cash flows, 146; subsidiary ledgers, 10

hierarchy, budget, 22-24
human resources office: in the consolidated budget, 29; department budgets, 25; expenditure forecasts, 101; payroll transactions, 137; position control, 42-45; in responsibility center management, 63; salary compression, 87

implementation plan, for strategic plan, 83-84
indirect costs: grant awards, 97-98; indirect services, 63-65; reimbursement of, 57-60, 63, 93; in responsibility center management, 63-64, 66; return on investment, 162-63
indirect services, 63-65
inflation, 101-2
Internal Revenue Service (IRS), 32
investments, 97, 163-64
invoice: and budget closing, 138-39; encumbrance, 16; trailing, 151-52

journal entries, 9-10, 140
journals, 9

lapsed salaries, 114-16
lease financing, 32-33
lease-purchase agreement, 33
ledger: definition of, 9; general, 10; posting to, 9-10, 16; subsidiary, 10
liabilities: in the chart of accounts, 14; definition of, 3-4; in the financial statements, 142-43, 145
line-item: auxiliary budgets, 39; budget format, 20-21; college budget, 28; consolidated budget, 29; expenditure projections, 100; incremental budgeting, 49-52; operating budget, 25-27; provost's budget, 29; rolling forward the budget, 52; variances, 122-23
liquidation, 16

margin, 156
market forces, 69-71, 94
money: insatiable demand for, 153-54; the power of, 153, 159; revenues and expenditures, 4

National Association of College and University Business Officers (NACUBO), 5, 92, 132-33
net assets: in the chart of accounts, 14; definition of, 3-4; double-entry accounting, 8; financial statements, 142-43
net revenue, 4, 141

operating budget: alignment with the strategic plan, 73, 83-84; and the capital budget, 35-37; closing of, 137-40; and the consolidated budget, 29-31; definition of,

21-24; and financial statements, 142-44, 146; hierarchy of, 22-24; implementation of, 110-22; modifications of, 123-30; preparation of, 89-104, 107-9; revenue allocation, 47-48, 104-7

participation fee. *See* participation tax
participation tax, 58-61, 64-66
political influence: on capital budget, 34; formula funding, 56; on state appropriations, 95
position: budget, 42-45; control, 42-45; number, 42-43, 115-16; vacancy, 44, 114-16
pre-audit close, 140
program reviews, 157-59
projections: expenditure, 100-102; flexible, 100; incremental, 93-98; revenue, 92-100, 104; statistical, 98-99
purchase order: budget adjustments, 127; closing the budget, 138-40; definition of, 16; in encumbrance accounting, 16-17

rebalance, 124, 160-61
recapture, 114-16, 124
repairs and maintenance: auxiliary enterprises, 39; capital budget, 34-35, 102; deferred, 37, 127; deficiencies, 34, 37; operating budget, 35, 102; priority of, 35; reserve accounts, 113, 124, 149
requisition, 16, 138
rescission, 124-26, 132
reserve: accounts, 113, 155; operating, 154-57; transfer to, 39, 113-14
responsibility center management (RCM), 62-68
responsibility centers, 62-64

retrenchment, 132-33
return on investment (ROI), 161-64
revenue: allocation basis of, 47-69; and base budget, 24-27; definition of, 4; forgone, 94; lines, 57; market forces, 69-72; projections, 92-100; restricted vs. unrestricted, 21-21

salaries: accounts for, 6-8; across-the-board increases of, 49-50; budget adjustments, 126-27; budget cuts, 135; budget uncertainty, 45; in college budgets, 28; in the consolidated budget, 29; in department budgets, 25-29; expenditure projections, 100-101; expense classification of, 5, 20; as an indirect cost basis, 64; indirect cost reimbursement, 98; lapsed, 114-16; personnel costs, 101, 147; position control, 43-45; release of funds, 112, 114; return on investment, 162-64; variances, 147; in zero-based budgeting, 48
salary compression, 87
salary savings, 114-16
scholarships and fellowships, 61, 94
scrub an account, 140
shared governance: strategic plan preparation, 76, 78; when downsizing, 133-34
sponsored projects financial reports, 150-52
sticker price of tuition, 94
strategic plan content: assumptions, 78-79; goals, 80-83; mission, 79-80; objectives, 80-83; values, 80; vision, 79

strategic plans: alignment with the budget, 73, 83–85; and the budget, 73–75, 83–85; buy-in to, 76–78; consultation, 76–78; faculty hiring, 87–88; implementation of, 83–88; implementation plan, 83–84; importance of, 73–75; leadership changes, 85; limitations of, 85–88; numerical targets, 81–83, 85–86; opportunities, 86–88; planning process of, 75–78; priority areas of, 73–77, 82, 85–88; specificity of, 77, 82–83. *See also* strategic plan content

subsidies. *See* subvention

subvention: allocation process, 59; of auxiliary budgets, 38–40; to balance the budget, 39–40; every tub on its own bottom, 69; as a grant, 65; as a loan, 38–41, 65; in responsibility center management, 64–66; in revenue-based budgets, 58–61, 105

sweep: fund balances, 149; operating reserves, 157

terminology conventions, 17

transactions: balance sheet, 142; budget adjustments, 126, 129; closing the budget, 137–38; definition of, 7; double-entry accounting, 7–11; encumbrances, 16–17; recording of, 9–10, 12–14; trial balances, 10–11

transfers: of authority to commit university money, 20; budget,

128–30, 149–50; definition of, 39. *See also* budget transfers

trial balance, 10–11, 140

tuition: account, 6; allocation of revenue from, 59; as an asset, 3–4; and bond debt, 32; discount, 61; and fees, 3–4, 93–94; financial aid, 61, 94; program closure, 134–35; return on investment, 161–63; sticker price of, 94. *See also* tuition revenue

tuition revenue: account, 6; allocation basis of, 59; vs. assets, 4; double-entry accounting, 7–8; and financial aid, 61–62; flexible budgets, 71; operating budget, 21; participation tax on, 59, 65

underallocation: for contingency funds, 113–14; definition of, 48; reserve accounts, 154–55

Uniform Guidance, 41

The Uniform Prudent Management of Institutional Funds Act, 96

variance: calculation of, 119; classifications, 119; definition of, 117; favorable, 119, 129; mitigation, 123–30; reports, 117–22; unfavorable, 119, 128; year-end, 146–47

windfall revenue, 123–24, 160

wisdom of the crowd, 105, 125